# Cavalletti

## for Dressage and Jumping

# Cavalletti

## for Dressage and Jumping

### INGRID AND REINER KLIMKE

TRAFALGAR SQUARE
North Pomfret, Vermont

This third edition published in the United States of America in 2014 by
Trafalgar Square Books
North Pomfret, Vermont 05053
www.HorseandRiderBooks.com

First published by J. A. Allen in 1969
Second edition published by J. A. Allen 2000
Reprinted 2015

Published simultaneously in Great Britain by J. A. Allen, London

Originally published in the German language by Franckh-Kosmos Verlags-GmbH
& Co. KG, Stuttgart, under the title Cavaletti

Copyright © 2011 Franckh-Kosmos Verlags
English translation © 2014 J. A. Allen

ISBN 978-1-57076-712-8

Library of Congress Control Number: 2014940892

Illustration credits
130 colour photos were provided for this book by Julia Rau/Kosmos.
Further colour photos are from the Klimke archives: page 8;
Julia Rau: pages 9, 24, 25, 27, 34, 91 (left and right), 92, 100, 139, 142, 143, 144,
149, 150, 152
Uviex Sports GmbH & Co. KG (1 photo): page 77.

Line drawings by Cornelia Koller
English translation by Claire Lilley

Printed in China by 1010 Printing International

# CONTENTS

## FOREWORD TO THE FIRST EDITION

The modern jumping seat goes back to the Italian riding master, Federico Caprilli, whose introduction of 'natural' training methods brought about a dramatic change to jumping style at the turn of the twentieth century. Prior to this, jumping was done with the rider's body leaning backwards and the horse's neck raised. Caprilli worked out that the horse could jump in better balance over obstacles if the rider leaned forwards and at the same time moved their hands forwards. These days this 'light' or 'forward' seat is universally accepted. Caprilli's programme included work over ground poles or 'cavalletti', which derives from Italian and means wooden poles raised off the ground with supports at each end. Caprilli used cavalletti to train the horse in different gaits, with and without the rider.

In Germany, the teachings of the Italian jumping school were slow to catch on. In the Kavallerieschule (Cavalry School) in Hanover, Oberst von Flotow was very interested in cavalletti work and through this made his mark in German riding history.

During the many years of my riding career, I have seen the importance of basic training. I was lucky enough to learn the value of cavalletti work at the Westfälischen Reit-und-Fahrschule (Westphalian Riding and Driving School) in Münster and from the various riding teachers I came to know at the Deutschen Olympiade-Komitees für Reiter (DOKR) in Warendorf. I learned more through putting this work into practice. I have had many high points during my lifetime: I have ridden event horses and dressage horses in competitions both nationally and internationally and I am sure that cavalletti work played a large part in my success.

Dr Reiner Klimke 1966

## FOREWORD TO THE 1997 EDITION

Many readers of this book on cavalletti work will hope to find some new inspiration. It is over thirty years since the first edition. The scepticism that many riders have had about schooling in this way has finally vanished. It is now clear that more progress is made in basic training with the use of cavalletti than without them and they are especially useful for gymnastic jumping exercises.

I am very pleased that my daughter, Ingrid, has come to the same conclusion as me, and includes gymnastic jumping in her own training regime. Ingrid has already had great success in riding at a top level in all three disciplines – dressage, eventing and show jumping. This gives the new edition a special value.

Dr Reiner Klimke 1997

## TRADITIONAL AND NEW EXPERIENCES

The origins of cavalletti work are in the 'natural' training methods and go hand-in-hand with the principles of classical riding, which my father followed and passed on to me. Cavalletti work is extremely valuable in developing the horse's athleticism and strength, while at the same time maintaining its health and wellbeing. Through training many, very different, horses for eventing at a high level and by following my father's training regime, I have fine-tuned these methods to suit today's 'sport horse'. This edition of the book includes many exercises and tips that are easy to incorporate into daily training. I hope you enjoy this book, and especially working with cavalletti!

Ingrid Klimke 2011

# CHAPTER 1

# THE VALUE OF CAVALLETTI WORK IN BASIC TRAINING

## Basic rules

I am not a fan of long theoretical explanations: I always find it difficult to discuss questions about basic training with people who know everything, but who have never sat on a horse. Nor am I a fan of riders who have no knowledge of basic training. However, there are riders – mainly in jumping – who rely on their natural talent, and do well despite having no basic training. Surely following systematic training will bring out the best in these riders? In other words, in my opinion, theoretical knowledge is essential for putting basic training skills into practice.

Many training problems can be solved far more easily if you do not rely solely on riding experience, but have a plan for how to go about the training before you start it. It goes without saying that it is imperative that every rider must have acquired a fundamental knowledge and an understanding of how to use precise aids before training can commence. In addition, you must take responsibility for the wellbeing of your horse. Only a healthy horse, whose condition and musculature have been carefully developed, can reach his full potential. The very best riders work in partnership with their horses and a partnership without responsibility cannot survive.

It must also be recognised that there is a difference between the loco-motion of the horse and riding as an art. Freiherr von Langen, one of the first competitors in equestrian sport after the First World War, was a great

Cavalletti work is a valuable stepping-stone in the basic training for the young horse.

believer in the idea that when a horse truly knows and has affection for his rider he develops 'self confidence and respect for his creator'. Langen's achievements were not only as a result of his equestrian knowledge, but also because of his demeanour and attitude. (In 1928, he won a gold medal in dressage with his legendary equine partner, Draufgänger.)

So, what does working with cavalletti bring to the training of horse and rider? What are they useful for? How can they be used for the best results?

## Why is cavalletti work useful?

When training a riding horse, the aim is to introduce natural gymnastic work. This is the way to ensure that his joints become more supple and his stamina and muscle tone improve.

The horse's way of going is totally dependent on his muscles and the contraction and relaxation of the different muscle groups is essential for strengthening them. Cavalletti work is very useful for this because it develops strength in particular muscles by asking the horse to move in a specific and controlled way. For example, the horse becomes more sure-footed as a result of lifting his feet high to go over the cavalletti and placing them back on the ground between the poles.

Riding over cavalletti builds muscle.

Cavalletti allow more demands to be made on the legs without compromising the quality of the gaits, namely walk, trot and canter. However, from the beginning of training, work on a horse's physical growth must go hand-in-hand with his psychological development. Cavalletti work must be systematic and gradually increase in difficulty. There is a risk of injury if cavalletti are over-used or if the layout of the poles interferes with the natural rhythm of the horse's gaits, so they must be placed carefully and work must be incremental. This is important because if a horse is encouraged to work when he is tense or in a forced outline, muscle growth can be affected, with the wrong muscles developing and others becoming fatigued or losing strength (atrophy).

Cavalletti work is also very useful for loosening muscles and relieving stiffness, especially with horses who have been badly ridden. For example, riding a horse over cavalletti with his neck lowered and stretching forwards and downwards will help specific back muscles to contract and relax, effectively loosening any tightness. The horse will quickly regain his natural rhythm. After only a short time he will take more weight on his haunches and become lighter in his forehand. His back will start to swing and the rider can just sit quietly in the saddle.

This horse stretches forwards and downwards over the cavalletti, working through his back in a relaxed way.

With rhythm and concentration established, the horse swings through his back, working confidently into the contact.

Cavalletti work helps to develop the strength required for forwardness.

Once you understand how to use it, cavalletti work opens many possibilities for improving the horse's suppleness and strength. It can be used to improve fitness since slowly increasing the amount and difficulty of the work increases the efficiency of the heart and lungs. Using cavalletti in conditioning work is particularly advantageous when you are developing a precise fitness regime.

Work over low poles also helps early schooling. One of the first challenges a young horse has is learning to balance with a rider on his back. By teaching him how to deal with this problem in a riding arena, you can prepare him for hacking out and jumping. As mentioned before, the training can be done in stages. Horses who have been ridden over poles become very sure-footed and quickly develop the confidence to jump over them. This work teaches them how to maintain their centre of gravity and develop a good sense of balance, which helps them to grow in confidence when they are ridden over uneven ground. Be aware that placing the feet precisely between poles takes concentration and is quite hard work.

Cavalletti work enables the rider to understand the psyche of the horse and learn how to bring out the best in him; it can even be used to train his intelligence. It can bring out the character and temperament of the horse – does he remain calm or become excited? Altering the layout and using different exercises that suit the specific horse can make a difference in his behaviour.

In dressage training, cavalletti improve the quality of the walk and trot in particular. Evenly placed poles can be used to work on the rhythm and regularity of movement, while having to step higher improves impulsion and cadence, which is a useful stepping-stone to training for passage.

> The usefulness of cavalletti work can be summed up as follows: **it is important for the basic training of all riding horses**. Cavalletti offer a wide range of training options and enable specific difficulties in any of the disciplines to be overcome quickly and easily.

## What does the rider learn?

Cavalletti work is invaluable for training the rider. Every sporting activity is done for pleasure, and that includes riding. If you want to ride well, you must have passion and proper training. It should go without saying that the passion needs to be nurtured for it to be long lasting, and often the nurturing comes from having a good riding teacher who explains why and how things should be done. For example, it is vital that each lesson has something new to inspire the students, and cavalletti work, with its huge range of possibilities, is often a good choice. There is nothing worse than going to lessons and repeating the same exercises week after week, without understanding why you are doing them.

This rider moves in harmony with her horse.

I have seen a vast improvement in young riders who are given simple exercises over cavalletti. These are so much fun that all stiffness and tension disappear, and the rider learns to ride in harmony with the horse in a very short space of time.

For example, negotiating cavalletti teaches the rider to sit quietly so as not to interfere with the movement if the horse stumbles or has any other balance problem. This is the exact opposite to what is learnt by almost every beginner, which is to lean back and pull back. In fact the hands must move forwards and the rider must go with the movement of the horse to allow him to use his neck to regain his balance. Suddenly sitting back in the saddle blocks the movement of the horse's back instead of freeing it.

When you ride over cavalletti it quickly becomes clear that to remain in balance with the horse, you must maintain a secure lower leg position by keeping the knees and lower legs securely against his sides. Maintaining balance by using a close contact with the knees cannot be practised too often and should be learnt from the start.

When cantering over low poles, the spring of the horse's canter stride is not as pronounced as it is when jumping over fences, so it is an ideal way to learn the basics of jumping. It also is a good way to acquire the feel of the horse swinging though his back.

More advanced riders can ride over low poles to perfect their seat; show jumping riders can improve their 'eye for a stride'.

> To summarise: cavalletti work is fun and a useful addition to the training of all riders. It improves the seat and the rider's 'feel' for the horse.

# CHAPTER 2

# PRACTICAL EQUIPMENT

## Different pole layouts

Cavalletti are poles made from wood or synthetic material. Both the ends of the pole are raised off the ground by supports. The poles should be thick, round and hard enough for the horse to take care when going over them. They should not split if they get knocked. The optimum length of the poles is around 2.5–3.5 m. The longer the poles, the harder it is to keep the horse straight when riding over them.

There are three common types of end support: rectangular, square or a cross. Generally speaking, rectangular supports are not ideal. Square and cross supports have the advantage that they can be set at three different heights and I prefer these latter two forms.

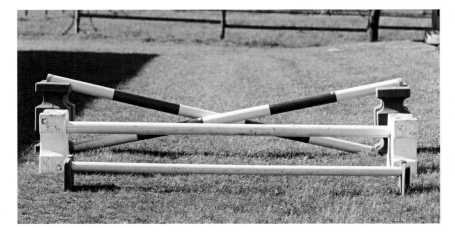

Different types of pole set-ups.

Cavalletti set at three different heights – 15–20 cm, 30–35 cm and 50 cm.

It is also important that the cavalletti are heavy so that they do not move very easily. I am not a fan of aluminium ones as they make a loud noise if the horse knocks them. This can be very alarming for a young horse, and even older horses tend to rush forwards at the sound.

The main advantage of plastic block supports is that they reduce the risk of injury. A young horse running out at cross-ended cavalletti could scrape a leg on them. Blocks are also easier to use when lungeing, as there is no chance of catching the lunge line on a cross end.

The lowest height of most cavalletti is 15–20 cm. This is best for work in walk and trot. The highest setting is generally 50 cm, which is ideal for canter because it encourages the horse to take care when going over them.

## Using ground poles instead of cavalletti

If you do not have cavalletti, you can simply use ground poles. Their drawbacks are that they are not at the ideal height of 15–20cm where the horse takes care over them and they can move if the horse knocks them. In addition it can be dangerous if a horse manages to stand on one that rolls, because it could jar the fetlock joint or damage a tendon.

You need between four and six ground poles or cavalletti. Young horses may benefit from jump wings or poles used as such. This will help to keep them straight when going over a sequence of cavalletti.

## Ground conditions

One of the most important things to consider is the condition of the riding surface – this is so often overlooked. In order to work the horse properly, the conditions underfoot must be good. Deep ground can strain

tendons and ligaments, while ground that is too hard has no cushioning for the joints and there is a risk of injury or jarring if the horse stumbles. The best surface is sand that is not too deep.

Cavalletti with poles used as wings.

If you have a choice between sand or grass, sand is better as there is less chance of slipping. It is important to set cavalletti on even ground without holes, so the horse can concentrate solely on going over the poles as this is the way to ensure he gains confidence and relaxes in his work.

## Equipment for the horse

I use bandages or boots to protect my horse's legs. Leg protection avoids the possibility of splints forming because of knocking injuries. I also use overreach boots if the horse is likely to overreach.

I do not use a different bridle or saddle for cavalletti work. However, it is important to use side reins when lungeing the horse to ensure a correctly rounded outline that will help to develop the right muscles.

# CAVALLETTI WORK WITHOUT THE RIDER

## Basic training in a natural outline

Now, we can get to work. It is undeniably important to train the horse and rider together as a partnership: on one hand, it helps the rider to develop a secure seat, which is fundamental for riding; on the other, it focuses on training the horse. In both cases, horse and rider learn to work in harmony with each other, developing trust and forming a true partnership. However, it is *liberating* for a horse to work over cavalletti without a rider. Without the rider's weight disturbing his balance, the horse will feel freer and more relaxed through his back; there is no danger of the rider touching him with a spur at the wrong moment or of their hands pulling him back.

What other reasons are there for working a horse without a rider? For a start, taking time over basic training and repeating simple exercises over and over again is the only way to progress, even if it seems tedious. It is also a chance to observe the horse. This enables you to get to know your horse's true character and disposition. You can watch his tail carriage, how his muscles work, and his movement in all three gaits – things you cannot see from the saddle. (Unfortunately, young riders rarely have the patience to spend time on this basic training. Maybe it is because they do not understand the importance of *observation* from the ground and how beneficial it is to ridden work.)

## Free-schooling

It is particularly beneficial to free-school horses over poles. Once a horse understands what is expected of him, he will enjoy it a great deal – and so should you.

To prepare a horse for any session of cavalletti work, lead him in hand in walk for about ten minutes, or ride him for ten minutes in walk. This is important for joint lubrication and to prevent strains or injury to the joints.

### Phase 1 – Free-schooling to loosen up

The horse should be tacked up with a bridle, saddle or lungeing roller, and without side reins. Place four cones in the school for him to work around. Allow him to run free for a while to work off any freshness (particularly if he has just come out of the stable), stiffness or tension. Uncontrolled charging around or stopping suddenly in the corners is not what is wanted, so it may be useful to have an assistant to ensure he keeps going around the school fluently.

If the horse is very excitable, it may be better to work him on the lunge rather than allowing him to run around by himself. Allow 5–10 minutes for a horse to work off steam before you calm him with your voice and prepare him for the work phase.

The horse should be allowed to run free to loosen up.

## Phase 2 – Working with side reins

The side reins maintain a consistent outline; the horse's back should be rounded and his neck stretching forwards and downwards. The reins should neither be too short, nor so long that there is no contact. They should be the correct length for the level of training of the horse.

It goes without saying that both side reins should be the same length to keep the horse straight, which is the opposite to lunge work. If the horse's neck is set on low with a large muscle on its underside, a triangular rein (*Dreieckszügel*) can be used. It should be positioned low on the girth to encourage him to stretch forwards and downwards.

Free-school the horse in the side reins, allowing him to trot and canter. After a while, he may start looking for support from the sides of the school, in which case, ask your assistant to keep him on the track. Use the four cones to encourage him onto the track as well. You may need two people to get him working in both directions.

It takes most horses about five minutes to start to work around the edge of the school. Some take longer. The calmer *you and your assistant* can be, the calmer the horse will be.

Free-schooling a horse gives you the opportunity to assess his character and intelligence, to see how willing he is and how quickly he picks things up. You must make sure you have a lot of *patience* – an essential quality for horsemanship.

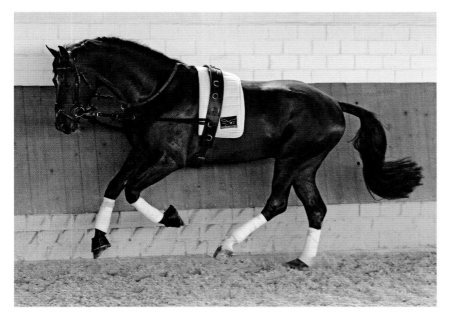

The beginning of the work phase using side reins.

Once the horse can maintain his balance around the school and is not looking to the wall for support, this phase of the work is complete and work over cavalletti can begin.

### Phase 3 – Trotting over cavalletti

*To be precise, a single raised pole is correctly called a *cavalletto*, but this form is not used in Germany and will be unfamiliar to most English speakers, so the plural form has been retained throughout.

With young horses it is very important to start with just a single cavalletti* and gradually build up to four. Set them at the lowest height, around 15–20cm. When you introduce two cavalletti, the horse may think it is a spread and jump over them. In this case, set the poles at double the distance, leaving a stride in between them.

Three or four cavalletti are best for trot work, so build up to this number as soon as possible. I do not recommend using more than four cavalletti as this can overface and unsettle the horse.

The most useful gait when free-schooling is the *trot*. In walk, the side reins can block the forward-stepping motion of the hind legs. It is also more difficult to keep the horse in a regular tempo on the track. Working without side reins when free-schooling has no value as there is no control over the movement of the horse's back.

In trot the distance between each pole should be 1.3–1.5m, no more than 1.3m to start with. You must work out the best distance for your horse.

Keep the height of the poles at 15–20cm, so the horse's muscles do not have to work too hard.

Work the horse in trot on both reins, going on his favourite rein first. In most cases, this will be the left rein. If you can, it is best to work in a small indoor school, rather than a large one, especially for lungeing, as this makes it easier to control the horse. Even with helpers, you will find there are challenges to working in a larger 60m arena.

Many people expect the horse to go over the poles steadily and calmly straight away and will discourage him from playing around and cantering past the cavalletti; however, this is not really a problem. If he goes into canter, wait until he settles down and comes back into trot by himself. A few quiet words are the simplest way to calm him.

Use cones and jump wings to prevent him from running out to the side. If the horse turns around or stops before the poles, it is best to trot him in hand towards them, and release him shortly before reaching them. This technique is particularly useful when you first introduce the cavalletti.

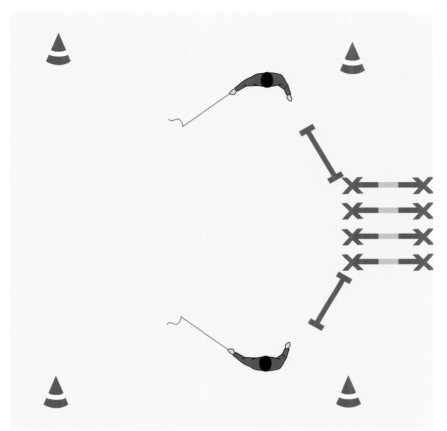

Cavalletti layout for free-schooling in the riding arena.

Side reins fitted correctly.

With horses who are familiar with cavalletti, trot work can start straight away. Try to keep the horse in a steady tempo. Experienced horses can become lazy once they have calmed down. To keep them moving, you may need to 'click', use encouraging words or flick the whip energetically towards them. Horses who are inclined to put a small step in between the cavalletti should be made to move with a bigger stride, covering more ground. Sensitive horses require very small driving aids; most move naturally forwards with plenty of energy. If you are a quiet, sensitive person with a good feel for the horse, you should be able to control the rhythm and speed easily and you'll find this very beneficial for your ridden work.

### Phase 4 – Increasing the distance between the cavalletti

Before the *distance* between the cavalletti is *increased*, the horse should be worked in medium trot on the free long side – the one without cavalletti. It is very important that his rhythm is not affected, so ask him to go smoothly into medium trot. Bring him back to working trot on the short sides by reducing the driving energy in the whip.

To begin with, the poles should be moved just a few centimetres further apart – the exact distance depends on the individual horse. The widest distance should be 1.5m. If they are too wide apart, the horse will have to put an extra stride in between them.

### Watch him while he works

Watch the horse for signs of how the schooling is going, namely:

▶ how energetic he is

▶ his expression

▶ the movement of his ears

▶ his tail carriage

▶ his breathing – look at his nostrils

Sweating is not necessarily a sign of fatigue. Look out for the other signs of tiredness. There is always something new to notice about your own horse; if you watch, you will soon start to be able to tell if he is tired and when he needs to have a rest. For example, in some horses dropping the tail can be a sign of tiredness. Look out particularly for him losing his enthusiasm.

Every successful attempt your horse makes to do as you ask should be rewarded with kind words. After several trots through the cavalletti, give him a *short break in walk* with a *change of rein*. The cavalletti layout should not be changed at this point, as the horse is already familiar with it and can work out the distance for himself when he is sent off in the new direction.

The time taken for a training session depends very much on the horse. It is just as important to spend time on stretching before doing any work. With a novice horse after, say, 10–20 minutes of preparatory work (that is the warming up and free-schooling with side reins), you might do a further 10 minutes of cavalletti work, followed by lengthening the strides a few times. Then the session should come to a close.

Remove the side reins and allow the horse to relax and cool down in walk until he is calm and his breathing has returned to normal, observing the movement of his nostrils and flanks. Once he has relaxed, he can return to the stable.

## How often should you free-school over cavalletti?

If you have the time and opportunity to work your horse every day, then he should be free-schooled over cavalletti once every 8 to 14 days. This allows for more frequent ridden sessions over cavalletti, as shown in the training programmes starting on page 131.

If you cannot work your horse regularly, it is still useful to school over poles, provided that every single lesson is carefully planned so it is of benefit to his training. However, it is important to remember that progress cannot be made with pole work alone.

Horses who are being trained for a specific purpose may need *specific schooling*. Event horses who work hard mainly over the summer months, can be kept in condition through the winter by trotting over cavalletti. I find this work beneficial too, since it keeps me fit and active during this lay-off.

My own regime is to work three or four times a week, with each training session lasting between 50–70 minutes.

## On the lunge

The benefit of working on the lunge over low poles is that it improves one-sidedness or stiffness in the neck and hindquarters. When he is bent on a circle, the inside of the horse becomes concave and the outside neck and hindquarter muscles must stretch (be aware that in some cases a horse may bend too much and become concave on one side). The inside hind foot takes more weight and steps forwards and under the body.

The length of stride can be altered by making the circles bigger and smaller without changing the layout of the cavalletti. For example, on one circle you can ask the horse to lengthen his stride and then bring him back to a working trot with a normal stride length for the next circle – this is another great advantage of working the horse in this way.

There are some things to watch out for when lungeing over poles: you need a lunge line about 7m long and the layout of the cavalletti will depend on the length of the lunge line. The size of the circle must be absolutely precise: alter the distance between the poles as necessary to achieve this precision.

The equipment needed for lungeing.

You must stand on the spot in order to lunge the horse correctly on a circle. You must also make sure the horse is responsive to the whip and rein aids.

Novice riders should use vaulting equipment for lungeing (i.e. a longer lunge line and longer whip) so the horse can be worked on a very large circle. Alternatively, they could free-school the horse over cavalletti, or ride over them initially, lungeing over them at a later stage. To simplify lungeing on a circle, just a single cavalletti can be used. Cavalletti with square or rectangular end supports are less likely to snag the lunge line.

## Cavalletti layout for lungeing

Lungeing on a circle over a single cavalletti is easy – simply place it on the track (at the middle of the short side of the school at A or C). If there are other horses working in the school, place it on the 'open side' of the circle on the centre line so as not to disturb them (i.e. at X in a 20 x 40m arena).

When the horse can happily work over a single cavalletti, both on the lunge and ridden, then you can progress to three or four poles on a circle. After a few circles, you will notice that the horse's concentration improves.

Cavalletti layout for work on the lunge.

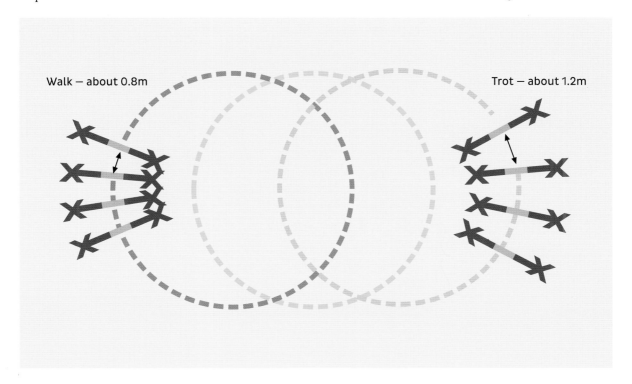

Walk – about 0.8m

Trot – about 1.2m

The aim of basic training on a circle is to improve the horse's way of going, and in my opinion the layout shown in the diagram on page 31 is the best. It does not need to be changed during a training session: the horse becomes familiar with the positions of the cavalletti, and this increases his confidence.

The middle circle (shown in yellow) is for lungeing without going over the cavalletti. The circle on the right (shown in pink) is for trot work, and the one on the left (shown in brown) is for walk. For safety reasons, the cavalletti are set on the sides of the circles nearest the short ends of the school. If you do not have eight cavalletti, six will do (with three on each circle) or you could use poles instead. It is important that the cavalletti are laid on the line of the circle – like the spokes of a wheel – so that they do not interfere with the movement and rhythm of the horse.

The distance for trot is between 1.2m and 1.3m, measured from the middle the cavalletti so that the distance is greater on the outside to allow for lengthening, or extending, the stride. They will be closer on the inside for shortening the stride. The best height to use is 15–20cm.

For walk, the cavalletti should be set so they are between 0.8m and 0.9m apart in the middle (where the horse will go over them). (Please note: the reasons against working on the horse's walk when free-schooling do not apply when you are using the lunge. This is because you have the lunge line and whip to help you control him and maintain an even, regular walk.)

## Phase 1 – Lungeing without cavalletti

Before lungeing over cavalletti, the horse must be warmed up. To do this work him on the lunge in trot or canter on the middle circle for about 5–10 minutes, either without side reins or with a light contact.

Most horses will be fresh to start with and may play around a bit. In this situation it usually helps to calm the horse with a few quiet words to bring him back into a steady rhythm. Asking for half-halts – by giving and taking a few times with the hand with the lunge line – can be useful for this. There are not many horses who allow you to work them straight away. It usually takes a few circles before they can be brought back to halt.

## Phase 2 – Attaching side reins

After loosening up the horse on the other rein for as short while, you can fit the side reins. It is important that he should already be used to

1 Lungeing before cavalletti work without side reins.

2 At the next stage with side reins attached.

working on curved lines. The inside side rein should be 5–10cm shorter than the outside rein. The outside side rein is used to control the amount of inside flexion and to support the outside shoulder, so its contact must be consistent.

The side reins should be attached so that they are level with the bottom of the saddle flaps, on both right and left sides. This is the same when working the horse on straight lines. This is the optimum height for encouraging the horse to 'chew' forwards and downwards into the contact. For lungeing, and free-schooling, a roller can be used instead of a saddle. This has the advantage that the side reins can be attached to the roller rings so they do not slip down, which can happen when attaching them to the saddle girth.

Be prepared to adjust the length of the side reins during a training session, starting with them slightly longer, and gradually shortening them as necessary.

There are different ways of attaching the lunge rein. I find it useful to attach it to the inside bit ring for both young and older, more experienced horses. One can maintain a much softer contact with the horse's mouth – the side reins ensure that there is no risk of the bit being pulled through the mouth.

A bit connector attached to both bit rings is useful if side reins are not used.

A third way of attaching the lunge rein is through the inside bit ring and under the chin to the outside bit ring. This, however, can be quite severe, and there is a risk of the horse flexing to the outside when lungeing on a circle. Even more severe is to pass the lunge rein through the inside bit ring and over the horse's head to the outside bit ring. I do not recommend this.

Another option is to attach the lunge rein to the bit ring and to the side ring on a drop noseband, which has a similar action to lungeing from a side ring on a lunge cavesson.

1 Attaching the lunge rein to the inside bit ring.

2 Attaching the lunge rein to the inside bit ring and the ring on a drop noseband

To begin with, the horse should be lunged in the side reins, using exercises such as transitions between trot and canter, on the middle circle in the arena, without cavalletti. Using aids with the lunge whip and your voice, the horse should be encouraged to relax his neck into the contact and to accept a steady contact with the bit. When he has done this on both reins for a total of 10–15 minutes, training over the cavalletti can begin.

## Phase 3 – Lungeing over cavalletti

The *young* horse must first learn to be confident over cavalletti. Start the first session with just one pole and allow him to go quietly over it. When he is working calmly, more cavalletti can be introduced, laid out as in the diagram on page 31.

Begin in trot with a tempo that suits the horse, and finish in walk.

After a short rest, during which the horse should be rewarded and the side reins adjusted for work on the other rein, repeat the same exercise, over the same number of cavalletti, on the other rein.

With horses who are already familiar to working over cavalletti, start with the layout on page 31. Begin by loosening up the horse on the middle circle, then start work over the outer circles. It can be a challenge to guide

This horse is relaxed and lowering his neck.

the horse from the middle circle out to the cavalletti while maintaining a steady rhythm and tempo. If this goes wrong, and the horse loses his stride, immediately bring him back onto the middle circle and re-establish a steady trot.

So, how do you *make the circle bigger?* Direct the whip towards the horse's inside shoulder at the same time as letting out the lunge line. You could also take a few steps towards the horse to encourage him to move away. Practise making the circle larger and smaller on the middle circle, before going over the cavalletti on the outer circles. Establish the trot work on the circle before trying to do this.

It is important to be aware that the horse's inside hind leg has to take more weight as it moves over the cavalletti. Watch that his fluency of movement is maintained. If he takes uneven steps over the poles, it could be a sign of tension or muscle pain – immediately return to the middle circle.

Even if the horse seems to be working quite calmly and happily, it is important that he should return to the middle circle after every 5–8 circuits of the cavalletti. Do a few circles in the middle then go back to the cavalletti. This adds variety to the training session. Horses take great pleasure in movement. It is your responsibility to nurture this and not to destroy it with monotony. Alternating between walk and trot, both over the cavalletti and on the middle circle, is the way to build muscle and to improve the horse's suppleness.

This horse trots energetically, but carefully, over the cavalletti.

Remember to *change direction* frequently to work through any stiffness. In my experience, a horse will relax much more readily if he is allowed to work on his easier rein for a while rather than being asked to concentrate on his more difficult rein.

The outer edge of the cavalletti circle, where the distance is wider between the poles, can be used when you are sufficiently experienced and skilful with the lunge line. As you both gain experience of this type of work, you will develop a stronger bond with your horse. Remember that as he learns what is required, he will need smaller aids and a lighter contact and this ensures that the work remains enjoyable; you will also find it is a valuable asset to your ridden work.

To summarise: **Work over poles should not exceed about 20 minutes in total.** Here is an example of a training session: 10 minutes in walk, 5–10 minutes working without side reins, 10–15 minutes working with side reins attached without going over cavalletti, and 20 minutes in walk and trot using cavalletti. The session should finish with the horse walking without side reins to cool him down before returning to the stable.

I do training sessions like this NOT more than every 8–14 days as it can be quite demanding for the horse, bearing in mind that ridden work over cavalletti is also being done on a regular basis.

# CHAPTER 4

# CAVALLETTI WORK ON STRAIGHT LINES WITH THE RIDER

## Basic rules

The aim of ridden work over low poles, with and without the lunge, is to make all ridden work easier. It is useful for the development of the horse as a whole and provides many training possibilities for the horse and rider, enabling them to build up their skills and go on to master quite difficult exercises. The starting point is to ride over cavalletti on straight lines.

## Various cavalletti layouts

Have a plan for each training session and decide beforehand which cavalletti layout will be most suitable for it. In my experience, there are five different types of layout.

The simplest arrangement is to lay several cavalletti on the long side of the arena – close to the wall of an indoor school or by the fence of an outdoor school – at right angles to the track. The advantage of this is that the horse simply has to continue on the track, so there is less chance of him running out to the side. Another advantage is that the rider does not need to pay so much attention to the horse and can concentrate on improving their seat. This means this layout is particularly useful for the less experienced horse and rider, helping them to build confidence.

A slightly more difficult layout is to place the cavalletti on the inside track. This has the advantage that the horse and rider do not have to go over the cavalletti on every circuit of the arena since they can go past

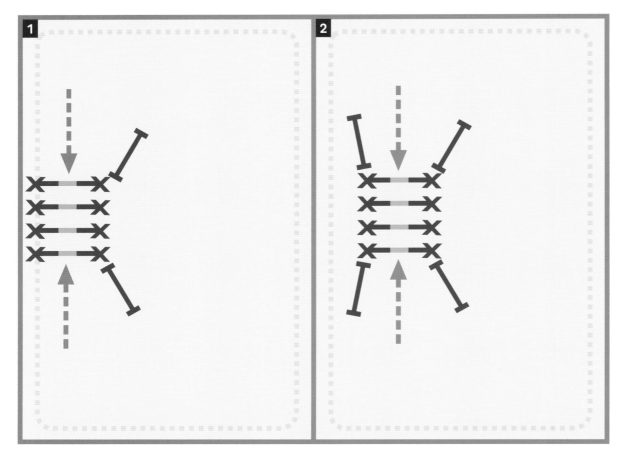

*Above*

1 Cavalletti layout by the wall.

2 Cavalletti layout on the inside track.

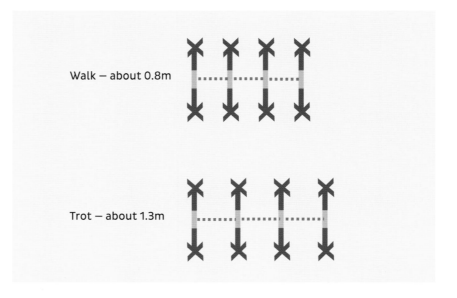

Walk — about 0.8m

Trot — about 1.3m

Cavalletti layouts for walk and trot.

them on the outside. However, you have to deliberately ride on the inside track to place the horse correctly for the cavalletti. It can be made easier by placing wings either side, which can be useful with a novice rider on an older horse, to prevent the horse from running out, but should not be necessary with more advanced riders and older, more experienced horses.

Another option is to place cavalletti on the centre line. I think this is very useful for changing the rein on the centre line, and for riding over the poles on both reins.

You can also set up the cavalletti for riding over them on the diagonals. In my experience, this is the most difficult layout to do. It is not that easy to place the cavalletti properly on the chosen diagonal of the school. However, it is worth trying because it is a good test of dexterity for young riders on experienced horses.

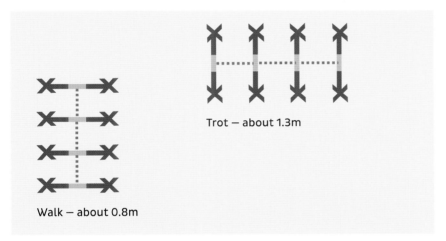

Cavalletti laid out for walk on the short side and for trot on the long side.

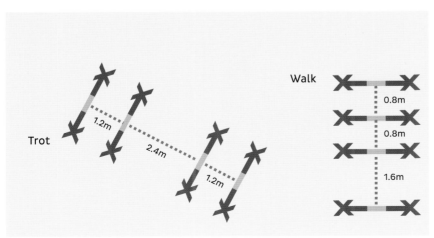

Layout variations for walk and trot with an extra step between the cavalletti. These layouts can be ridden from either side.

Ideally, it is best to have separate layouts for both walk and trot, so there is no need to make any alterations during a lesson. It is a matter of personal preference whether to lay the poles near the track, or nearer to the centre line. Finally, it is the responsibility of the trainer to choose a suitable layout to suit every horse and rider in the lesson, although, of course, advanced riders can choose a layout to suit themselves.

## Cavalletti work in walk

The *first time a horse is ridden* over cavalletti it should be in walk, as this is the gait in which the horse is most balanced. Start with a single cavalletti and give him a loose rein, but make sure you ride with enough forward motion, using your voice as necessary.

At the second attempt, the horse should understand what is required and not need to be driven so much.

The rider's upper body should be inclined slightly forwards, to minimise the risk of disturbing the horse's back should he jump. If the horse remains calm, a second pole can be added at a distance of about 0.8–1m after the first, then a third, and a fourth, and so on, up to a maximum of six in a row.

I have often seen horses tense up when they are presented with several poles in a row. It could be that too many have been added too soon. The answer is to reduce the number of cavalletti and take the horse over these

Cavalletti with a stride between them laid out for walk. The horse is ridden on a light contact. His front line could be a bit more vertical.

until he is calm. Then increase the number of cavalletti, but this time more slowly.

If horses are already familiar with cavalletti, they can be presented at a whole layout straight away. It is important to ride *on a long rein* at first so the horse has the freedom to balance unhindered. You should also check the distances between the poles and adjust them if necessary.

Walking over poles that are set at the correct distance follows the natural sequence of the walk, with each hoof placed on the ground individually as follows:

1. Right fore

2. Left hind

3. Left fore

4. Right hind

One of the problems that is said to be a possibility with walking over poles is that the horse 'paces', moving the right fore and right hind together, and left hind and left fore together, so losing the four-beat rhythm of the walk. However, I have never actually seen this happen; most horses find a comfortable rhythm.

With correct riding, all the gaits can be improved. We will now distinguish between medium walk, collected walk, and extended walk.

1 Medium walk on a loose rein.

2 Here the horse is slightly crooked.

3 It works much better with a contact.

### Medium walk

Medium walk must be ridden with a soft flexion at the poll and a contact with the bit. The rider maintains the contact with steady hands while using the driving aids – the back and legs – to keep the impulsion. This gives control over the length of the stride. The hind feet should slightly overtrack the prints of the front feet.

Once the horse has lowered his neck and willingly accepts the contact he can be ridden over the cavalletti: the length of the stride can be achieved by setting the correct distance between the poles. The hands should be kept as low as possible. At about a horse's length before the cavalletti, the rider's hands should give a little in the direction of the horse's mouth to make sure the horse is in balance. The rider should also lean slightly forwards to lighten the seat. If this is done correctly, the horse will reach forwards and downwards with his nose and allow his back muscles to relax as he steps over the poles.

It is not always easy to maintain a soft contact with the bit. Many horses stiffen their neck, tighten their back and go against the reins. In this situation, try the following correction: ride a circle or a figure of eight before the cavalletti and try to bend the horse to help him to soften and to give to the aids. After bending him, ride straight to the cavalletti, encouraging him to 'chew' the reins forwards and downwards from your hands. In most cases, the horse will relax the back muscles and stretch his neck, lowering his head. Reward him with a pat on the neck after each successful attempt. Repeat the exercise a few times and finish on a good note.

> The most important points that the rider should be aware of are:
>
> 1. Ride straight.
>
> 2. Ride forwards.
>
> 3. Ride the horse with a low neck carriage, light contact and low hands.
>
> 4. Follow the movement of the horse with the upper body.

Try to ride calmly and in balance as you approach the cavalletti. If you do not ride straight, the horse may fall out of rhythm and then the distances between the cavalletti will become wrong. A clumsy approach

will also unbalance him and make his steps uneven. Suddenly dropping the contact may frighten him, making him reluctant to stretch forwards and downwards. Conversely, holding your hands too high with a hard contact, and using the seat too strongly, will make him lift his neck and hollow his back. I emphasise, *the rider must not lean back* with the upper body when approaching cavalletti – if they do, the horse will not be able to relax his back. The driving aids should be the lower legs and the voice, not a strong seat. If you use a whip, use a short one on the horse's shoulder. Using a schooling whip behind the leg or on the haunches can make you lean back slightly.

Walk on a loose rein showing total relaxation and softness through the back.

## Extended walk

Extended walk is essentially a 'bigger' version of a medium walk. The hind feet should step far over the prints of the front feet. The rider must allow the horse the freedom of his neck but without losing the contact

Riding straight over the middle of the cavalletti.

with the mouth altogether. When you attempt extended walk without cavalletti, there is a risk that instead of the horse's frame lengthening, his strides become short and hurried. This can be avoided by practising frequently over cavalletti set at exactly the right distance. It is vital that the reins are given forwards when going over the first pole. This will encourage the horse to stretch forwards, 'chewing' the reins from the rider's hands.

The distance between the cavalletti should be increased to around 1m, depending on the length of the horse's stride. If the horse cannot make the distance, use firmer driving aids on the next attempt. Because of the increased strain on the muscles, tendons and ligaments when riding extended walk over cavalletti, this exercise should not be repeated more than ten to fifteen times.

## Collected walk

Collected exercises should be done in the last part of the riding lesson, once medium and extended walk have already been attempted.

In correct collected walk, the hind feet step just behind the prints of the front feet. Each individual step should be higher, landing with more pressure on the ground. The horse's neck should be arched and raised. The forehead and nose should be on the vertical.

For collected walk, the distance between the cavalletti should be put back to 0.8m again and then closer still, depending on the horse. The cavalletti should be placed at their middle height of about 35cm. After riding over them between five and ten times, it is a good idea to change the rein by riding a half circle at the end of the long side of the school and then returning to the track, while allowing the horse to stretch and to 'chew' the reins from your hands.

Riding collected walk is the hardest exercise in dressage. Over and over again, horses resort to pacing instead of collecting. This is because they are driven too fast, and thus lose the four-time rhythm of the walk. The reins are then shortened. The horse misunderstands the rider's aids, and simply walks faster and higher, losing the sequence of the gait. I find cavalletti help me to avoid this problem.

With cavalletti, the horse has to make the walk steps higher because of the poles but he cannot rush, so the four-beat rhythm of the walk remains secure. Riding the horse on the bit with shorter reins ensures the neck is correctly raised and arched over the poles.

Remember that it is very important to ensure every cavalletti exercise is executed well and with precision. When this is done, this work helps horse and rider to train in the right way. It can help the rider notice when things are going wrong and prevents them from riding without due care for the horse. The precision required to ride cavalletti helps to develop the physiological and psychological aspects of riding, and emphasizes that riding is an art.

Medium walk on a long rein with a light contact.

## An exercise in balance

It is quite common for young horses to trip, and work over cavalletti improves their balance. It helps them to learn from the outset to be sure-footed and self-reliant, and to realise that there is no outside force to save them. It is particularly important that this is learnt before teaching a horse to jump, when mistakes are far more dangerous.

As preparation for jumping and cross-country, I use the following uneven distance exercise in walk and trot. It helps a horse begin to learn how to balance over uneven ground – sure-footedness is important for all horses – and can improve alertness in more experienced horses. Set

This rider is in harmony with her horse's movement. The reins and her forearms form a straight line.

the cavalletti at the correct distance for walk or trot and then remove the middle one from the row so that the horse has to take a stride without going over a cavalletti. There are many variations on this theme that can be tried, such as removing a different one from the row or altering the height of the cavalletti.

Always take great care with this type of work, since injuries can be caused by training for too long or when the rider does not give the horse enough support. A tired horse can easily overreach or knock his legs.

How often schooling in walk over ground poles is done depends on whether the rider has time to ride every day. An ideal is once or twice a week in winter, and once every 8–14 days or so to fit into a training regime. (See page 131.)

## Cavalletti work in trot

If the horse started his training by being ridden over cavalletti in walk, he should be quite used to them by the time trot work commences. Again, start by using a single cavalletti, then gradually build up to four.

The distance between them should be 1.3–1.4m. The optimum height is about 15cm.

If the training of both *horse and rider* has been established in walk, there should be no problem in going on to work in trot. There is, however, a difference between schooling the young horse and training the young rider. A novice rider should be trained on an experienced

An experienced horse gives a youngster a lead.

Rising trot with a low hand position.

horse. An inexperienced rider working on their own with a young horse is bound to get into difficulties.

### The light or forward seat

I think cavalletti work is invaluable for all riders and every horse, no matter what stage they are at, and one of the most valuable exercises for the rider is to trot – and later canter – over the cavalletti in a light seat. This seat is the best way to allow the horse to find his balance in preparation for both show jumping and cross-country. The rider leans slightly forwards and takes their weight through the thighs with the knees closed tightly against the horse's sides and the heels pressed down. This gives a secure lower leg position and eases the horse's back. The stirrup leathers should be two to four holes shorter than normal. The hands should remain still and low either side of the withers. This position is well known and should be taught by every good riding instructor.

Trot work in a light seat over cavalletti consists of three distinct exercises.

The first exercise is simple. It is just to improve the rider's confidence and to help them to cope with all eventualities. Establish a steady trot and lean slightly forwards just before the cavalletti, holding the mane with

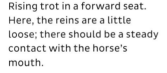

Rising trot in a forward seat. Here, the reins are a little loose; there should be a steady contact with the horse's mouth.

your hands. Once you feel confident and balanced in this position, take your hands forwards in the direction of the horse's mouth.

The second exercise is a little more difficult. The aim is to practise keeping the knees close to the saddle. To do it, you have to stand in the stirrups when going over the poles. You can hold the mane until you are more confident in your position and can manage to keep you knees in contact with the saddle, maintaining a secure lower leg. To keep your balance you should allow your leg joints to flex with the movement of the horse. After a few repetitions, and once you are balanced, you can stop holding the mane and take your hands forwards in the direction of the horse's mouth. You can put your inside hand on the horse's neck to help with your confidence if necessary.

Once you have learnt to stand in the stirrups in balance with the horse's movement, you can move on to the third exercise, which is to learn to relax the arms and to develop an independent hand position, without relying on the reins. Aim to keep your upper body forwards as you go over the cavalletti in rising trot, without falling back behind the vertical and without your hands going up and down as you rise up and down. This balanced seat is the foundation for galloping and jumping.

## Sitting trot

Another exercise that helps the rider to get the feel of the horse's back swinging is to ride over the cavalletti in sitting trot. It also helps develop a balanced and independent seat. If the rider is experienced enough to remain in balance and can feel the movement of the horse, they can fine-tune their awareness of the horse's back as it swings, or can feel if it tightens under them.

It is easy to damage a horse's back by doing sitting trot over cavalletti without due care, so this exercise should only be done on experienced school horses or by good riders who are at the stage of teaching their horses passage (see page 57), since the trot steps should be shortened and ridden in a tempo that is comfortable for the rider to sit to.

## Working trot

The trot is a gait with a two-beat rhythm where the horse springs uniformly from one diagonal pair of legs to the other. The different types of

Working trot, sitting in the saddle. The cavalletti have one stride in between them.

trot are working trot, collected trot, medium trot and extended trot. *The schooling of a horse's trot* over cavalletti should begin with working trot.

In working trot, the hind feet should step into the hoof prints of the front feet. The horse should be in a good rhythm, without tension and with energy. The most important thing is that his back must swing, with fluid movement from behind and without carrying weight on the forehand.

It takes more effort for the horse to trot over cavalletti as he springs from one diagonal pair to the other and the work helps to develop the strength of the back muscles. For this reason, riding in a light forward seat with the horse in a lowered neck carriage is ideal. The lower the horse can stretch forwards and downwards over poles, the more his back can round. The best back-strengthening exercises allow the horse to 'chew' the reins out of the rider's hands or to stretch forwards and downwards on a long rein while mouthing the bit in a relaxed way.

## Trotting challenges

This type of work is often much more difficult to do properly than you might expect. If it is not going well, it can be quite hard to find out what is wrong, especially if the horse seems to have difficulty working in balance with a lowered neck position.

Here are some possible causes and solutions. Many horses speed up when they see poles, preferring to canter over them rather than trot. Keep a horse like this in working trot by using half-halts, and prevent him from taking hold of the bit by giving and taking the reins.

Horses who are worried often raise their noses in the air over poles; they will also tighten their backs and become hollow and out of balance. If they do not calm down after a short while, go back to working over just a single cavalletti. This usually works well, especially with sensitive horses, and avoids the risk of injury.

Many horses like to raise their heads on the approach to see what is in front of them. However, when they actually take off over a jump or go over cavalletti, they voluntarily lower their necks and raise their backs. In this situation, do not try to prevent the horse from raising his head as this will cause resistance, and he will very quickly lose trust in you.

In most cases, the reins are better too long than too short so a horse does not feel restricted by the rein contact. Forcing him into an outline

This horse is behind the vertical and the contact is too tight.

will only cause resistance and tension. Rewarding him by patting him or by stroking his neck will reassure him and make him relax.

When you are trying to establish a steady tempo, it is important that the horse does not become too slow or crooked. Use the driving aids to bring a lazy horse back into balance.

Other causes of problems may be neck and jaw issues, sensitive backs or tensing against the contact in response to bitting problems.

Horses with a problem about accepting a contact should be schooled without cavalletti at first to teach them to work into the contact and to trust the rider's hands. This requires a great deal of knowledge and skill on the rider's part. Work on circles, voltes and serpentines to encourage the horse to relax through the back. Once he seeks the contact, lowering his neck, and is able to work in a steady rhythm, cavalletti work can recommence. A longer warm up, with plenty of bending exercises, will help to keep this type of horse relaxed. Initially, simply aim for him to trot calmly over the cavalletti; sometimes it helps to ride voltes, halt or rein-back before the first pole.

Problem situations are always somewhat unpredictable: every horse is different and will not necessarily react in the same way each time. Above all, you must be confident and brave. If the horse is misbehaving, you must try to keep a quiet contact with the bit. If you can do this

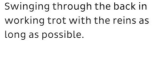

Swinging through the back in working trot with the reins as long as possible.

Riding in a steady trot, going with the horse's movement with the upper body slightly forwards.

once or twice, it is only a question of time before the horse accepts it more readily. This is down to the horse trusting the rider, and the rider's self-confidence. After a few training sessions, the horse should able to be ridden normally without him becoming stressed. Using cavalletti in conjunction with loosening work will fix many problems much more quickly.

If you start off well but the strides become irregular during training, this is a sure sign that something is wrong. It could be that too much has been asked of the horse too soon, and he is showing signs of discomfort or being tired. In this instance, immediately go back to some easier work to end the session on a good note.

Important points *for the rider* when trotting over cavalletti are:

1. Ride straight.

2. Maintain a quiet, but not lazy tempo.

3. Keep the hands low and have a light contact with the horse's neck in a low position.

4. Lean slightly forwards to keep in balance with the horse, and ride in rising trot where possible.

After a few successful exercises in working trot, the lesson can either be brought to a close, or training on improving the different types of trot can start.

### Lengthening the strides in trot

Medium trot has energetic steps with a longer stride than working trot. The horse lengthens his frame in order to cover more ground. For this reason, the distance between the cavalletti should be widened to between 1.3 and 1.5m. The rider should be in a light seat with a soft contact. The horse should be asked to 'lengthen the strides' two to three strides before the first cavalletti. It is important that there is enough space on the approach to the cavalletti for the horse to establish bigger steps. If the trot is too fast, there is a risk of him running and he may become tense, and either break into canter or lose his rhythm in trot by suddenly shortening before the first pole, and then leaping forwards again.

This exercise helps to teach the horse how to maintain a precise tempo, while the rider gets a feel for the length of their horse's strides, which helps them do develop 'an eye for a stride'. For this reason, it is a very beneficial exercise for show jumpers and eventers.

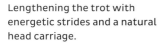

Lengthening the trot with energetic strides and a natural head carriage.

The best way to develop the power and swing needed for *extended trot* is to build up to it systematically from medium trot. However, I ride extended trot without poles to reduce the risk of injury and to ensure my horse remains happy in his work.

## Passage

I have successfully used the following exercise to prepare several horses for passage. Set the poles at 35cm high and ride the horse in collected trot over them. This will encourage most horses to perform the correct action for passage, which is to take higher steps; the exception being horses with naturally flat gaits. Riding passage-like steps over cavalletti is a good way to correct uneven steps behind. The distance between the poles must be sufficient for the hocks to bend in conjunction with the haunches, in rhythm. When doing this exercise beware that there is a danger that the horse will push his hind legs out behind, and try to passage through excessive movement in the haunches and dropping the croup.

This is valuable *preparation work* for the passage and, of course, it is an exercise for advanced horses and riders.

I am fully aware that this advice may be disputed, as there are very few riders who teach their horses passage in this way. In fact there are many

Giving with the inside rein while riding passage-like steps over cavalletti.

Mouthing the bit in a relaxed way at the end of the training session.

riders who are against training dressage horses through using cavalletti. But I think cavalletti really are useful as preparation and correction of passage. I find it very sad that many dressage riders concentrate so much on exercises such as half-pass, flying changes, canter pirouettes and so on that they run the risk of forgetting the true aim of dressage altogether.

> The aim of dressage is that the horse, through systematic gymnastic training, is made more beautiful and powerful and his natural movement is improved.

It is rare to see horses warming up for dressage in a relaxed way, with a loose, supple back and with their noses beyond the vertical. It is hardly surprising that such tense horses have tense strides and little co-ordination, which results in them being unable to spring off the ground evenly in the passage.

I reiterate that cavalletti should only be used to *improve the passage* once a horse is established in the basics and can move in a relaxed manner. If this is not the case, the horse will be tense and unsettled over the cavalletti. As always, it is important to not use more than four cavalletti in a row.

A cadenced trot over cavalletti with a step in-between.

When first considering whether to use cavalletti to train passage myself, I was worried that my horses might have leg problems, but this fear has been unfounded. I have never had an injury working a horse in this way. I think it is down to taking regular breaks during training sessions. In every case, taking time to establish the work and always making sure that the horse's strides are even and fluent is the way to achieve your goals. It is down to the rider's experience to choose one exercise over another, and it will vary depending on the horse and the level of training.

## An exercise in concentration

As described for walk (see page 48), the horse's concentration in working trot can be improved by arranging a row of cavalletti set 1.3m apart and then removing one from the middle of the row. Have the cavalletti at their lowest setting. I do not recommend raising them to 35cm at any point for this, as the horse may be wary, and you might risk a fall or losing the horse's trust.

Ride forwards enough to achieve a balanced trot over the poles. The in-between step (over the missing pole) should not be ridden as a shorter step as this would interrupt the horse's rhythm and may make him stumble.

Trot work over cavalletti should follow on from walking over them. The length of time spent in training should be 15–20 minutes in trot with plenty of short breaks, usually taken when something has been done well. For fitness training, the training time can be extended to 30–35 minutes. Further details can be found in the training programme starting on page 131.

## Cavalletti work in canter

Riding in canter over cavalletti is no different from grid work – jumping over a row of small fences set at related distances. Canter is the horse's fastest school gait. One differentiates between right and left lead canter according to which foreleg is leading. The canter is a three-beat gait with a slight pause, called the 'moment of suspension', when all four feet are off the ground. The leg sequence of the canter is as follows:

1. outside hind

2. inside hind and outside fore

3. inside fore

4. moment of suspension

(In the gallop, the second phase of the canter sequence is split, making it a four-beat gait.)

There are four types of canter: collected, working, medium and extended. If the rhythm is lost, the canter becomes disunited: the leg sequence is faulty and there are now four beats:

1. outside hind

2. inside hind

3. outside fore

4. inside fore

A correctly ridden canter has powerful steps with a clear moment of suspension. Each canter stride should be clearly recognisable, free-moving and lovely to watch. In my opinion, cavalletti work really improves the canter – for dressage horses, too.

Working over cavalletti improves fluency and increases the activity of the haunches, encouraging the hindquarters to tuck under. The canter

stride then has more push, or impulsion. Using cavalletti is also beneficial for teaching horses who are straight but have problems taking more weight on the inside hind leg during the canter strike-off.

An exercise that has positive results is an 'in and out' or bounce jump on a circle. For this, four cavalletti are placed on a circle. The distance between the cavalletti will be greater on the outside, and less on the inside, to a degree dependent on the length of the cavalletti and the size of the circle. The rider canters a circle, going over the 'in and out'. The rider is responsible for the rhythm, and the accuracy of the circle line. Through this exercise, the horse learns better balance, developing more power and engagement. After a successful attempt, do not forget to take a break in walk on a long rein, with plenty of praise! Cavalletti training in canter is strenuous work for horses who are new to it.

Working over poles in canter is also very beneficial for loosening. Canter is the favourite gait of horses with a lot of Thoroughbred blood, so they loosen up easily in canter. Of course, the horse should be warmed up in all three gaits.

More details of including this work in a training programme start on page 131.

*Above left*

The inside hind foot steps far under the centre of gravity. The rein contact could be more consistent.

*Above right*

One can also canter over cavalletti in a dressage saddle in a light seat.

# CHAPTER 5

# CAVALLETTI WORK ON CIRCLES

## Preparation

Riding over cavalletti on circles and half circles makes a welcome change for young riders. The horse should already have sound basic training and be used to working over cavalletti on straight lines. When working on both straight and curved lines, the horse must be straight. This means that the hind feet must follow the tracks of the front feet. On circles, the horse is not straight if he makes the common fault of lifting his hind legs and moving them out to the side rather than stepping forwards under the centre of gravity. In order to avoid this, he must be flexed to the inside.

Cavalletti work on circles and half circles helps to loosen the horse, and can rectify stiffness on one side or the other, so the horse bends and flexes equally in both directions. If a horse is not straight, he will often lose rhythm – this where cavalletti work can help by restoring elasticity and encouraging the placing of the hind feet under the centre of gravity.

Over poles, the horse does not have the chance to step out to the side with the hind legs. The length of stride and placing of the feet is so precise that the horse maintains rhythm by himself. It takes very little practice before the hind feet step into the tracks of the front feet.

There are two main types of layout: circles laid out in the same way as for work on the lunge (see page 31). The upper diagram on page 65 shows cavalletti set on a middle circle. In this way, the circles at each end of the school, the track, the diagonals, and the centre line are free, which enables more than one rider to use the school at the same time.

Cavalletti work in trot on a circle. Fluid, powerful steps into a secure contact.

This horse has a powerful, ground-covering trot, which means he is comfortable on the outer edge of the circle. Horses who cover less ground should go nearer the middle.

The lower diagram shows a layout for a figure of eight, the idea being to work the horse equally on both reins. Each circle requires four cavalletti set in a fan near the short side of the school. It is important to leave the track free so you can ride around the whole school on the track. In trot, this exercise is known as 'changing direction through the circle'. It is not as useful in walk as it is in trot, but it is best to ride it in walk to start with and you can revert to walk if you get problems, too.

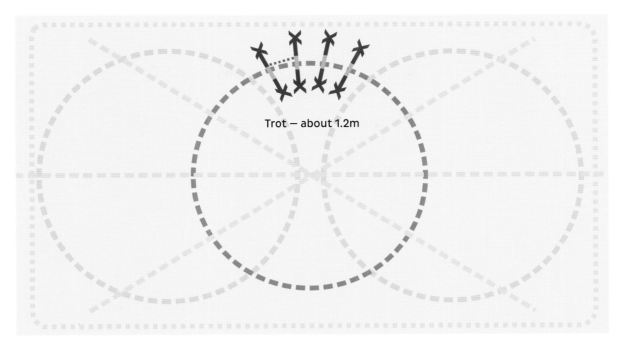

Cavalletti on the middle circle, leaving the circle lines,
the track, the diagonals and the centre line free.

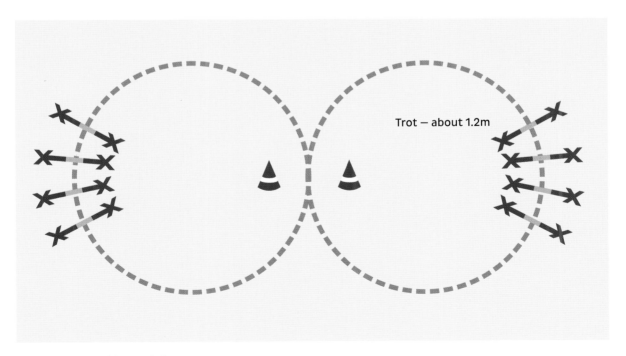

A figure of eight with two circles
the same size.

Layout for trot and canter work on a circle: the rider trots over the trot cavalletti, canters at the cone, canters over the canter cavalletti and rides a transition back to trot at the next cone.

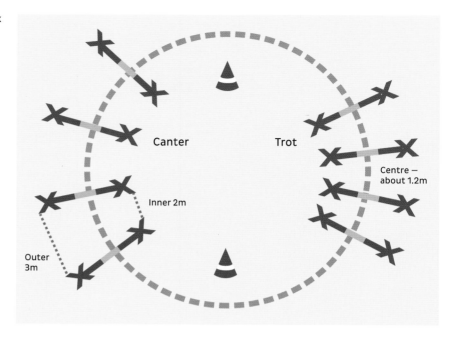

Riding over cavalletti on circles is especially beneficial for training the horse's inside hind leg to take weight. Because of this it can be quite strenuous, so avoid doing it for too long. Always tailor schooling sessions to the stage of training the horse has reached.

The work can be divided into four phases.

## Phase 1 – Loosening up exercises

This is about preparation. It should include loosening up exercises in all three gaits and a few trot exercises over poles on straight lines.

Allow the horse a short rest while the cavalletti are set out on the circle. You can avoid a major reorganisation by arranging the cavalletti beforehand – for example putting four of them on a straight line parallel to the track on the long side and four on a circle over the centre line. However, in the end it's a matter of what you find easier.

## Phase 2 – Work on circles

The second phase consists of the main work on circles. Keep sessions brief – always take account of how the horse is coping.

Do working trot on the circle, making sure your seat is light. Just before the cavalletti, move your hands slightly forwards, and ride exactly

A lovely example of self-carriage on a circle. The inside hand gives forwards.

over the centre of the cavalletti. If the horse stays on the aids through the cavalletti, the direction can be changed, and the same exercise ridden on the other rein. If cavalletti are set on one circle only, then a change of rein can be made '*through the circle*'.

It is best to begin on the horse's better rein before changing to the more difficult rein. I find this helps the horse since he will be likely to relax on the better rein and then work willingly on the more difficult one.

The aim is to work the horse evenly on both sides, to work on lateral bend and suppleness through the ribs.

After working on the circle, do some exercises on the straight: ride forwards on the long sides to re-establish freedom of movement. Riding forwards always has a place in training when overcoming stiffness or resistance.

The master of dressage Gustav Steinbrecht famously said, **'Ride the horse forwards and make him straight.'** Every rider should always bear these words in mind.

Horse and rider are working in harmony. Notice the contented expression of the horse.

When riding the circle the next time, ride over the centre of the cavalletti again. On each subsequent circle, make the circle bigger, moving out to where the cavalletti are wider apart, so the horse has to stretch more, making his steps bigger. This means that the inside hind foot must push off the ground with more energy and at the same time take more weight.

At this point it is easy to cross the boundary between training to build muscle and straining muscles. For this reason, this exercise should only be repeated a few times, riding each circle just once in each direction every time.

### Phase 3 – Finishing on a good note

The third phase is gradually bringing the work to a finish. It is important to ride some easy exercises that the horse is familiar with at the end of the session. He will then return to his stable happy and relaxed and will come out calm and willing to work the next day.

Finishing on a good note makes work the next day twice as easy. After working on circles a few times, allow the horse to stretch and 'chew' the reins out of your hands.

Riding over cavalletti on circles is very useful for improving the rider's seat and for developing 'feel'. You will even feel the benefit when riding on straight lines because it helps to develop a secure, balanced seat.

Riding instructors should use their experience to choose exercises that are helpful in basic training. Above all, cavalletti should be 'fun' for the rider, but this type of work must only start when the rider's seat is secure. There must never be any danger of injury for either horse or rider. Young riders in particular appreciate alternating between exercises in straight lines and circles. They often start to see the work from a different perspective and come up with their own ideas.

Both horse and rider show total concentration on the exercise.

# GYMNASTIC JUMPING

## Introduction

The first part of this book was primarily about training methods and exercises aimed at building a solid foundation, which is very important for successful jumping training later on. The second part looks at using cavalletti for gymnastic jumping and for training young riders as well as young horses. You may wonder why there is such a distinction between training the horse and the rider – but in my experience this is the best way to fully understand individual aspects of basic training. As horse and rider learn to work together, they learn to trust each other and to work as a true partnership.

During my father's long career, I had many lessons with Fritz Ligges, having been recommended one of his books. When I trained abroad in Canada and America, I had jump training with Ian Millar, and learned his training methods. I had further training under Anne Kursinski, who had a great deal of influence over my own riding technique. This part of the book makes use of all the techniques I have learnt over the years. It covers all aspects of jumping: from jumping for the first time with a novice horse to building up to gymnastic jumping, and includes many practical tips to help with training along the way.

Gymnastic jumping is excellent for improving the relationship between rider and horse. It covers a wide variety of schooling areas that are relevant to all the disciplines – dressage, show jumping and eventing – and for both horses and riders.

Jumping in harmony with good style.

At the end of this section are examples of training programmes. They provide a broad outline of what to include and can be adapted to suit the individual rider and horse.

Hopefully, you will gain an understanding of the value of gymnastic jumping *throughout* basic training. I believe it is important not to specialise in any one discipline too soon.

Gymnastic jumping is the best way to introduce a sequence of jumps, and the skills learnt can be used to jump a course at a later stage in the horse's training. It is just as important for the dressage horse throughout his basic training as it is for the jumping horse and rider.

## Basic rules

Gymnastic jumping is about schooling the horse over cavalletti, poles, small jumps and doing grid work to improve suppleness and concentration. Through this, both rider and horse gain the confidence and experience required to tackle a full jumping course. Gymnastic jumping is a great way to really get to know the horse and to ride effectively.

The exercises are devised to help the horse to think for himself. This means that the rider must interfere as little as possible, but support the horse when necessary.

On a practical note, the obstacles should be between 60–100cm in height, and the horse should wear leg protection – bandages or boots.

The jumps may be small, but they are very effective! The way they are set out is very important. Monotony and boredom can be avoided by using a variety of jumps set at different distances.

It is important to tailor the jumps to the individual horse and rider partnership. This is a good way to avoid problems from the start. Remember that most issues can be put right with care and praise – this is the way to develop trust between rider and horse from the beginning.

Always wear an approved safety helmet – these days there are as many varieties of hard hat as there are styles of jump!

## Aim

Improving the horse's athleticism by riding over poles, cavalletti and doing grid work has the added advantage of improving the skills of the rider. The two must work together as a team – not as two individuals. By using different exercises, great progress can be made in a short period of time.

The aim of grid work, or a series of jumps in a row, is that it helps the horse to stay straight, leaving the rider free to concentrate on their seat. Learning to *go with* the horse is the way to improve balance and develop a secure and supple seat, which, in turn, is the foundation for asking the horse to work properly though his whole body.

Grid work also helps to improve *concentration and co-ordination*. The jumps follow closely one after the other, and teach both horse and rider to react quickly. With grid work, the horse is encouraged to jump in a rhythm. This teaches the rider how to feel for the *length of the horse's stride,* which is needed later on for establishing a good tempo in the canter.

As the distances are clearly defined in a grid of fences, grid work also teaches the horse and rider a feel for the *stride between each fence.* This helps them to become more self-confident and established in their work. Both learn to trust their instincts.

Every exercise should be carefully planned so that both the rider and the horse gain in self-assurance and neither is over-faced. It is also vital that every lesson finishes on a good note. They will then both enjoy the work.

An important aim for gymnastic work over fences is to improve the *suppleness and strength of the back muscles of the horse.* It is very important to build the jumps in a sympathetic way with an easy stride pattern – suiting the natural stride length of the horse – so the horse can relax and use

Varied obstacles increase the horse's concentration. The height of such jumps is not critical.

his back in the right way. When building jumps for a novice horse, there should be a ground line in front of each jump to help with taking off at the right place. This can be gradually moved closer to the fence, and later removed altogether.

By working him through a variety of exercises, you can teach a horse to think for himself and this allows him to relax. You must also teach him how to look out for himself when under pressure. For this reason, it is important to change the layouts on a regular basis. For example, a horse can be trained to react quickly by regularly altering the distance between the fences. Short distances teach horses to take their weight behind, and to step under their centre of gravity. Wider distances encourage them to jump with a longer stride and with more confidence. Jumping bounces requires energy, and also develops dexterity and strength in the hindquarters. Again, it is important that the distances are set to suit the horse: a youngster will more quickly learn to work in balance if the distances are correct – more so than jumping single fences – but he will soon get into difficulty if the distances are wrong. If this happens he may become unbalanced and find the exercises too much to cope with.

Bounces develop the power of the haunches.

## Planning a schooling session

Every training session must be systematically and progressively planned. The rider or course builder must have a goal in mind, and this should be built up step by step through the lesson. For example, to prepare the horse for grid work, the canter should be shortened at first, to help the horse find an optimum stride length. It can also help to ride over a single fence in the arena as preparation, so the horse takes off at the correct place and in balance, stepping under behind. (It is important that the horse does not 'stand off' at the fence.)

It is down to the individual how much emphasis is put on grid work in the training programme for both rider and horse. As a rule, one should work two or three times per week over cavalletti or jumps. For young horses it is better to do a couple of short exercises four times a week, or to incorporate them into dressage schooling. Do not try to do everything in one training session in a week, but do a little at regular intervals; an exception is horses being trained for dressage: it may suit them to have just one weekly session.

Stretching forwards and downwards in the loosening up phase.

The main phases of a training session are:

1. Loosening up

2. Working phase

3. Relaxation

They consist of:

1. At least 10 minutes in walk on a long rein, which can include walking over cavalletti, 15–20 minutes loosening up in trot and canter, working around the fences. Riding over cavalletti in trot is super-loosening work.

2. About 10–20 minutes jumping (gymnastic jumping exercises, building up the work step by step). Riding dressage in between, or having short breaks in walk depending on the ground conditions and the temperament and training level of the horse. The total time spent riding over cavalletti or small jumps should be no more than 15 minutes. The rider should learn to recognise when the work phase should come to an end, and the relaxation phase should begin.

3. To finish with, the horse should be worked in trot with a lowered neck position, 'chewing' the reins from the rider's hands. This should be followed by allowing the horse to walk on a long rein, stretching forwards and downwards for at least 10 minutes. A short hack in walk is good relaxation for both rider and horse.

A successful training session is one that is carried out calmly, and with plenty of reward – and never in a hectic or hurried way.

## Equipment

As stated before, the rider (all riders, not only beginners) should always wear a safety helmet. It must be properly fastened by its chin strap. Other equipment for jumping is a whip and, for more advanced riders, spurs.

Novice riders should ride without spurs until they have developed a secure lower leg position. In normal circumstances, advanced riders should always wear short, blunt spurs in case the horse ignores the leg aids. Spurs help to teach the horse to be more sensitive to the leg.

A safety helmet.

In my opinion, if you have a horse who is 'behind the leg', it is more effective to use the whip than spurs. The whip should be a mid-length one. Short whips usually make the rider's hands move about far too much, interfering with the horse's mouth, while longer whips are more useful for touching the hind legs to increase activity rather than behind the leg to reinforce the leg aids.

For novice riders, a safe, experienced horse is vital. He should be so well trained that he will help the rider out of difficult situations if they make mistakes. Such 'schoolmasters' are very hard to come by, but they are the best way to give the rider a good foundation.

## The basic elements of riding over fences

Before the rider begins jumping over fences, they must have a *sound, basic dressage training* so that they have their horse properly 'on the aids'. They must be totally confident in their ability to use the aids independently (for example, they must be able to rise to the trot without the hands going up and down as well). They must also be effective enough in their use of the aids that they can stop the horse easily.

The horse must fully accept the rider's aids and must respond to the transition aids without the rider having to resort to the overuse of the whip or spurs.

Jumping over cavalletti builds trust between rider and horse.

The rider must not be afraid and must be looking forward to the first exercise. Any tension and stiffness will make it hard for them to learn the feeling of how the horse moves when jumping. If the rider *trusts* the horse, the riding instructor can start with some simple exercises (cavalletti or poles laid on the ground, which will be explained shortly).

Self-discipline and concentration are the keys to the rider acquiring skills in their riding lessons. They must learn to focus on their seat and weigh up the best approach to each fence. They must also follow the horse's movement, without disturbing his balance. When these things come automatically, they can start to concentrate more on other skills.

Both rider and horse learn by repetition. Through repetition, fluidity of movement and feel will become second nature, as can rhythm and tempo. Along with thinking about their seat, these are the most important elements for a rider to be aware of. There are various ways to improve these, too; for example, counting the strides between fences can develop regularity in the canter.

I have said it before, but in my opinion it can't be repeated too often, each exercise should be divided into three phases:

▶ A warm up phase

▶ A jumping phase

▶ And a cooling off phase

All the phases are equally important for successful training of both the rider and horse.

Many riders use up a lot of energy riding towards a fence only to lose concentration after it, meaning that they have an awful lot to do to prepare for the next obstacle. When jumping a course, the strides immediately following a fence should be ridden as the preparation for the next.

The most important requirements for achieving a harmonious, stylish jump that is done with a correct seat and in balance (which are explained in more detail on pages 81–6) are:

▶ The ability to think ahead

▶ An energetic tempo

▶ An even canter rhythm

A good seat, rhythm and the right speed are the three most important requirements ...

... for successful jumping over fences.

In the beginning, the rider should concentrate on one thing at a time until all the skills become automatic; this is the same for everything a rider learns.

The rider must keep the horse in a *steady tempo* and select the best approach to each fence. They must leave the horse alone over the fence so he can think for himself. Many riders are unable to keep the canter rhythm on turns. When the rider *can* turn towards a jump with the correct canter tempo (achieved by shortening and lengthening the stride), the horse has enough time to concentrate on the jump. With the right tempo, he can canter in balance, maintaining rhythm towards the jump. As the rider shortens the canter stride, the horse collects and stays under control. An energetic, ground-covering canter is not the same as a fast canter that is out of control. When you watch top riders do this it looks easy, but it takes practice.

In brief, the rider is responsible for three things:

1. They must take a good line of approach

2. They must maintain the correct tempo, or speed (and an even rhythm)

3. They must keep the horse on the aids (and not fold forwards at the wrong moment)

This young horse has spooked at the 'water' under the fence and jumps higher than necessary.

> I like this phrase: **Canter on in the turns, sit in balance and rhythm, ride forwards to the fence!**

As soon as the rider has the feel for the length of the canter stride, they will be able to work out the optimum tempo for their horse and this allows them to see the strides between fences.

On the approach to the fence, the rider must keep the horse on the aids, in balance and with the right length of stride. (This applies to curved, as well as straight, lines.) The rider must work out if the distance to the fence is to great or too small, and react quickly to lengthen or shorten the canter stride accordingly to reach the optimum take-off point. They should be able recognise in advance if the approach to the fence is wrong and to make the necessary adjustments (without

panicking and riding too fast at the fence). They need to get into the routine of seeing a stride throughout their training until it becomes automatic.

When riding corners between jumps, the rider must maintain the tempo and plan the approach to the next fence.

## The jumping seat

In show jumping, you see many interpretations of the classic jumping or light forward seat, where the rider is sitting lightly in the saddle and almost upright. Every experienced rider will their own individual style; the most important thing is that they are secure in the saddle and can adapt their technique to suit a variety of horses.

Here are the elements of a good jumping seat:

▶ The rider's upper body should lean slightly forwards from the hips.

▶ In the bascule over the fence, the rider should lean sufficiently forwards with their seat far enough out of the saddle to maintain balance with the horse.

▶ The rider must sit in balance over the horse's centre of gravity.

▶ The rider's weight is taken on the thighs, knees and ankles.

▶ As with the dressage seat, the heels should be the lowest point, but with the feet a little further into the stirrups (on the balls of the feet).

▶ The knees must be more flexed: keeping the knees firmly on the saddle gives the rider the necessary security.

▶ When landing, the rider should keep the heels down sufficiently to prevent the lower legs swinging back – the calves should be in line with the girth.

▶ The upper arms, elbows and hands should work with the upper body.

▶ The forearms and reins should form a straight line to the horse's mouth.

▶ The hands should move in the direction of the horse's mouth, allowing the neck to stretch forwards.

▶ A soft contact must be maintained between the rider's hands and the horse's mouth.

▶ The rider should look straight ahead between the horse's ears.

A lovely sight – rider and horse in balance.

## Upper body

To clarify a few points: when riding in a light forward seat, the *upper body* must swing slightly with the movement of the horse. The rider should remain in balance with the horse and the movement of the upper body should be minimal so as not to disturb the rhythm. In order to sit lightly on the horse's back, freeing up the back muscles, it helps to imagine 'kneeling' into the saddle.

A common mistake is when the rider leans too far forwards with the upper body, and 'jumps before the horse' (getting in front of the horse's movement), which means the rider's weight falls over the forehand. This scenario makes it much more difficult for young horses, who are not so balanced, to make a good jump. With youngsters the canter is not 'uphill' enough for the hind legs to be under the centre of gravity, so if the rider leans too far forwards, the horse has to carry this additional weight on his forehand. The rider should sit quietly on the approach to the fence and take off in balance with the horse. It is equally important not to lean forwards too late as this will mean they are 'left behind', hindering the horse's movement on take off.

One way to correct this mistake is to do some jumping without stirrups.

The rider should also concentrate on looking forwards between the horse's ears. By this I mean they should be focusing on the next obstacle. If the rider does not look where they are going soon enough, they cannot plan the line of approach to the next fence. When riding a related distance between fences on a curved line, the rider should think about *riding the line as a whole*, and not by jumping each fence in isolation.

To reiterate:

▶ Look towards the fence early enough to plan the line of approach.

▶ Directly after the fence, plan the approach to the next fence.

## Leg position

The position of the lower legs is very important when jumping as it determines the balance and position of the upper body. The heels are the lowest point on the rider. The legs should always be in contact with the horse's sides (again, not too far forwards nor too far backwards). It is easier to keep the calves against the horse's sides if the toes are turned out slightly. The rider's weight is supported with flexible knees and ankles.

*Above*

This rider has a balanced seat, even without stirrups.

The rider is correctly focusing on the next obstacle.

The leg contact should be soft: the rider should not be gripping too tightly. If this happens, the horse will go against the aids, and become 'dead to the leg'. He will not react quickly to the rider, which is very important when jumping a course.

## Hands and arms

The hands must move forwards as the horse goes over the jump, and remain forwards on landing.

The *arms* move forwards – not the upper body! They should give sufficiently forwards and downwards to allow the neck to stretch, whilst maintaining an elastic contact with the horse's mouth. Novice riders should move their arms forwards and hold onto the mane with the hands, using the horse's neck for support. It is far better that the reins are a bit loose, even losing the contact over the fence, than it is to pull on the horse's mouth.

Advanced riders should know their job and be able to jump well even without reins at all, which I think is a very good way to improve the seat.

This is more difficult – jumping without reins or stirrups.

This horse is showing good front leg technique over the fence.

Commencing trot work: riding over the middle of the cavalletti.

After the jump, the contact should be regained, with both hands still going with the horse's movement (and not pulling back!) Sometimes, as a precaution, it is useful to rest the hands on the crest of the horse's neck for support. This gives more control should the horse make an unbalanced jump or throw up his head on landing. A good rider can adapt their hand position either towards the horse's mouth, or towards the neck as necessary. They can also keep their own balance independently from the horse!

## Exercises in cantering over cavalletti

### Exercise 1 – Cantering cavalletti on straight lines

This exercise helps the rider to practise getting a feel for the horse's movement while in a light, forward seat, as well as establishing a rhythmic canter and getting used to the length of the horse's stride.

Place a low cavalletti in the riding arena so it can be ridden on both reins. Stick a wide band of tape around the centre of the pole so the rider is accustomed to riding over the middle of obstacles from the beginning.

In walk, the rider should practise riding straight towards the middle of the cavalletti, and continue to ride straight afterwards.

Next, the same exercise should be ridden in *rising* trot, making sure the rhythm and tempo of the trot do not alter at all.

From the beginning, the riding instructor should make sure that their pupil is looking towards the cavalletti early enough. As they go over the cavalletti, they should be looking forwards.

Remember that the landing phase is as important as the take-off.

The rider should concentrate on keeping a straight line over the cavalletti every time. This is easy to do if the horse is straight in the first place.

Once the horse is able to trot over the cavalletti in the desired way, canter work can begin.

The most a horse will do over a low cavalletti is make a bigger canter stride, so the rider should be able to maintain a light seat and ride quietly without fuss. The first easy jump is made up from the following four phases:

▶ A straight approach

▶ Riding over the middle of the cavalletti

▶ Cantering straight on afterwards

▶ Keeping straight when coming to a halt

Transitions into and out of walk and trot can be ridden frequently during the exercise to maintain interest. Changes of rein are also important and should be done regularly.

Next, the cavalletti can be turned to its greatest height and the whole exercise ridden in canter, so the rider gets used to the feeling of the horse jumping a small obstacle. An experienced horse will just take a bigger canter stride, in the same way as over the cavalletti set at the lowest height, maintaining the same rhythm. Once the rider has done this exercise correctly a few times, they can take a short break in walk to relax.

Turn the cavalletti back to its lowest height and set a second one five canter strides away. The length of a horse's canter stride reckoned as 'normal' for these exercises is 3.5m, although this does depend on the ground conditions and the height of the fences. Allow one canter stride for the take-off and landing phases combined. With a small jump, the take-off and landing phases are short, so 19–20m should be sufficient. This means that the horse canters at a normal tempo over the first cavalletti, and takes five strides, before cantering over the second.

First, the rider should trot over both cavalletti in rising trot. They should stay on a straight line, and also halt on the straight line. Once this can be done on both reins, the same line can be ridden in canter.

Once the rider has learnt to jump small cavalletti, they can progress to higher fences.

A good halt on a straight line after the cavalletti.

As always, it is important that the rider has a correct light forward seat, is supple enough to follow the horse's movement, and looks ahead to the second of the cavalletti. If the pair can maintain rhythm and stay on the straight line, the cavalletti can be turned to full height and the exercise repeated.

If the rider can ride a transition to halt from the canter after the second of the cavalletti, more variations can be added, such as a change of rein through a circle, a simple change or voltes. Again, the exercise should be done on both reins.

The horse should always be waiting for a halt transition. This indicates that he is truly on the rider's aids, which is very important when riding a course.

Once the rider has succeeded in riding two small jumps on a straight line, they will also have learnt to canter in a rhythm and will have established their light forward seat. And all this has been done in their first experience of jumping.

When they are familiar with the first exercise, the rider can try counting out loud the five strides between the cavalletti without including the landing phase, which is a common mistake (often made by novice riders). One should count the first stride after landing (1,2,…5) and try to maintain the canter rhythm. It helps if the instructor joins in to begin with. The normal (suitable) tempo for each individual horse should be established before turning onto the straight line of approach, and should remain constant right until the halt after the second jump.

Counting the canter strides has the effects that the rider learns to feel the rhythm and to calculate distance. After a few times, they should recognise that when they count 'three', they are *two* strides from the second jump. Then they will learn to *see* when there are two strides to the second jump. This exercise helps to develop 'an eye for a stride', which is the ability to assess whether the current tempo will mean that horse is able to maintain harmony and rhythm over the fences, or whether he needs to be ridden more forwards, or be collected.

## For advanced riders

This exercise is also useful for *advanced* riders who wish to acquire a better feel for their horse's stride. It can also be used to experiment with the length of the canter stride – taking four or six canter strides, which means shortening or lengthening the canter strides accordingly.

This rider is looking straight ahead over both cavalletti.

First, the advanced rider can ride the distance in four strides by increasing the tempo. The rider should already be able to lengthen the canter strides in their dressage work. If this is the case, they should be able to ride lengthened strides over the cavalletti.

The increased tempo should be established before riding the line of approach, so the strides are already lengthened before the first of the cavalletti. After landing over the first, the four rhythmic canter strides should come automatically as the rider rides the horse forwards. The rider should be able to ride in a light forward seat, maintaining rhythm and keeping a soft contact with the horse's mouth, and continue over the second cavalletti.

Nest, they can try to collect the canter and ride the distance between the cavalletti in six strides.

As always, the preparation for this should have been done in their dressage training when working on altering the length of the canter stride. To do this, it helps to sit in the saddle with the upper body upright.

Ideally, the canter should be collected well before the first cavalletti, so that the six non-jumping strides come automatically. On landing, if the rider realises that the canter stride is not collected sufficiently, it must be shortened more (which is easy to do – just sit in more and close the hands).

The exercise is brought to a close by halting on the straight line.

### Exercise 2 – Cantering cavalletti on a circle

This exercise works on improving several skills. The rider establishes their light forward seat. They get a feel for rhythm and a suitable tempo for riding on a circle. Bending is good gymnastic work for the horse and improves the quality of his canter. Possible problems when a horse is jumping on a circle include changing the canter lead and falling out. To prevent this from happening, the rider should make sure that the horse is flexed and bent to the inside. They should also maintain a steady canter on the circle.

Put one cavalletti at its lowest height on the circle. The exercise is to jump this cavalletti on a circle. It is helpful for the novice rider to set the cavalletti on the track at the short end of the school, on the closed side of the circle (i.e. the side of the circle nearest the wall). This prevents the horse from running out. This exercise should be ridden in trot first to make sure the circle is ridden accurately, i.e. it is round.

It is amazing that there are so many riders who cannot do this simple exercise correctly. Many riders do not plan their line of approach soon enough nor look where they are going around the circle line. These are all skills that should be taught properly from the beginning.

The exercise should be ridden on both reins, so it is worked equally in both directions. The rider must canter over the middle of the cavalletti. To finish with, a few circles should be ridden on both reins in a light forward seat to practise cantering in rhythm.

If the exercise has been successful with the cavalletti at its highest position, as well as its lowest position, on the closed side of the circle, it should be tried with the cavalletti at the lowest height on the open side of the circle. This is much harder than you think as the circle line must be maintained before and after the cavalletti.

This rider is cantering over both cavalletti on a circle. She looks towards the next jump without unbalancing her horse.

Once again, the cavalletti can be raised when the rider is confident with the lower height. An experienced horse will naturally take a bigger canter stride over the cavalletti without speeding up.

To make the exercise more difficult, two cavalletti can be used, one on each side of circle. Again, this should be ridden in trot to start with, at the lowest height.

It is important here to think about the key aspects of the exercise: the rider must look immediately towards the next cavalletti after going over the first.

Two of the benefits of looking forwards to the next jump are that it gives the rider no time to think of anything negative and prevents them from looking down at the jumps. This is how to become a forward-thinking rider.

A rhythmic canter over three 'bounce' cavalletti on a circle.

If the rider rides accurately in trot without any problems, both cavalletti can be ridden in canter. Once both cavalletti can be ridden at their highest setting, on both reins, the rider should continue until they can ride in a regular rhythm on the circle over the middle of both the cavalletti each time.

Riding this simple exercise well is a good indication that everything is correct and that the rider has developed a good feel. The horse learns to jump a second fence without getting over-excited or speeding up. There should be frequent breaks throughout.

## For advanced riders

An advanced rider can take this basic exercise further. A variation is to ride a figure of eight, changing direction over a single cavalletti. Once again it is important to start the exercise in trot. Two equal-sized circles should be ridden.

Another variation, still using simple movements, is to change the rein through the circle.

Remember that every time the rider wants to change the rein after going over the cavalletti, they must look in the new direction.

When changing the rein through the circle on the figure of eight, two cavalletti should be used, one on the outer side of each circle. A change of rein can be ridden in trot, with a simple change or with a flying change. This exercise helps the rider to teach their horse to be attentive and responsive to the aids, having to concentrate on both cavalletti and the change of direction.

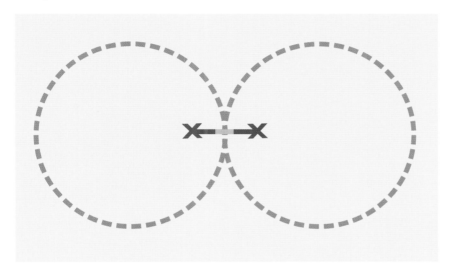

Changing direction over a cavalletti
by riding a figure of eight.

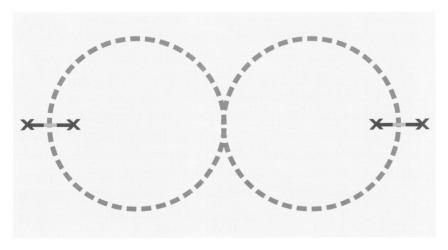

Riding a figure eight with two cavalletti –
one on the outer side of each circle.

Another variation is to place four cavalletti evenly spaced around the circle one at every quarter. A helper is useful to set the cavalletti out quickly. The rider must make sure they look forwards to each of the cavalletti in turn. This improves reaction time as the jumps come quickly one after the other. The circle must be maintained. The rider must also maintain the horse's flexion, bend and rhythm over the cavalletti to prevent him from changing canter lead and running out. The challenge is to do this in an even rhythm. If the horse speeds up, he must be steadied with half-halts. The aim is to ride around the circle with the same number of strides between each of the cavalletti. After a few circles, rider and horse will find a steady rhythm and get the feel for the stride most comfortable for the horse when cantering on a circle.

After a few successful circles, the rider should take a break in walk, and repeat the exercise on the other rein.

The next stage is to ride on the inside track over the cavalletti (see the diagram below). This requires only three canter strides. Riding on the outer track requires four canter strides. The aim of this exercise is to learn how to maintain either three or four canter strides between the cavalletti. Advanced riders should be able to alter the number of strides between each.

Four cavalletti placed equally around a circle. The inside track requires three canter strides between the jumps, and the outer track four strides.

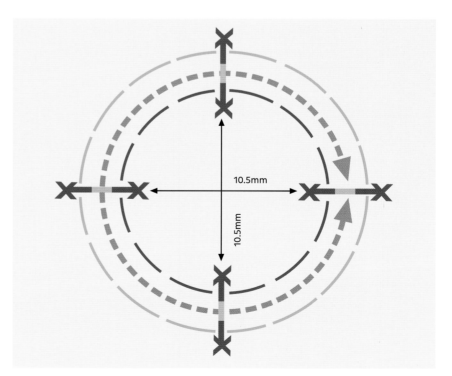

10.5mm

10.5mm

At a later stage, small jumps can be used instead of cavalletti and again it is useful to have a helper near each jump to put up poles if they are knocked down, or to raise or lower them.

Once this exercise and its variations have been completed, the rider should be familiar with the light forward seat or jumping seat. This is good grounding for jumping over grids and related distances. Simple layouts for jumping are given in 'Grids for novice horses' (page 103).

## Typical mistakes and their solutions

This section is mainly for advanced riders who have ridden for some time, but developed a few bad habits (usually owing to a lack of good instruction on improving their seat). Because these riders have a particular way of riding ingrained, they will have to concentrate very hard to get used to the feel of a new way of riding. It always takes time to correct faults. It is necessary be self-critical in order to get rid of long-term habits, and it takes time before new feelings become second nature.

Cavalletti work is particularly useful for correcting the seat.

The examples are not aimed at the novice rider. Novices need to grasp a good understanding of the seat from the beginning and this is the responsibility of the riding instructor, who should correct shortcomings as soon as they occur. You need a correct seat to be able to influence and support the horse with effective aids.

Riding over a series of cavalletti highlights the rider's faults without overstressing the horse. Once the rider has corrected their jumping seat over cavalletti, the next step is to consolidate the seat by gymnastic jumping by way of grid work.

The rider must concentrate very hard on improving their seat, so they do not have to repeat the exercises too many times. This avoids the horse having to do too many jumps and becoming bored and perhaps careless as a result.

### PROBLEM >

The rider does not look forwards over the jump; instead, for example, looking down at the neck.

### CORRECTION >

The riding instructor, or helper, should stand in line in the middle of the jumping grid, at some distance, holding up a number of fingers on one hand.

This rider is looking down at the jump and twisting his upper body.

While jumping over the line of fences, the rider should look at the raised hand, and call out loud the number of fingers that they can see.

If the rider is schooling alone, they can pick a reference point of some sort, such as a letter of the school or a fence post, to look at instead.

### PROBLEM >

The rider does not look in the direction of the next obstacle soon enough.

### CORRECTION >

For this, use a simple grid with one or two strides between the jumps.

The rider should practise looking to the left when jumping the first fence, look to the right over the second, to the left over the third, and to the right over the fourth.

This helps to establish a secure, balanced seat and heightens concentration (by speeding up the reactions). The rider should be supple enough to turn their head back quickly to look straight over the next fence without losing balance.

### PROBLEM >

The rider leans on the horse's neck for support on take off and/or landing.

### CORRECTION >

Jumping without stirrups and with the hands either on the hips, folded behind the back, or out to the side prevents the rider from leaning on the neck with the hands.

Again the exercise should be ridden over a simple grid. The reins should be knotted to prevent them from getting hooked around a front leg. To start with, the reins can be dropped on the horse's neck just before the last fence in the grid. At each attempt, the rider should let go of the reins a fence earlier, until the whole grid can be ridden without reins. If doing this exercise in trot, the reins should be released over the first fence or cavalletti.

The rider must have complete faith in the horse, trusting that he will be obliging and jump straight. This exercise also tests to see if the horse has the ability to jump without the support of the contact.

There is another exercise that helps the rider to develop independent hands and practise giving forwards with them over a jump. Over each successive jump the rider should move the hands forwards along the crest of the mane, then towards the horse's mouth, and then, finally, have their hands forwards and wide apart, not touching the horse's neck

*Left and below*

The rider places their hands on their hips and maintains balance while jumping without stirrups or reins.

at all. By doing this, they will develop independent hands, but this does require them to have a secure, balanced seat.

**PROBLEM ❯**

The rider is unbalanced.

**CORRECTION ❯**

Jumping without stirrups.

The best way to improve balance, for both dressage and jumping, is by riding without stirrups.

This rider is not in balance and is in front of the movement – 'jumping before the horse'.

*Below*

This rider has a balanced and supple seat and is jumping without reins or stirrups.

Riding without stirrups is an easy way for the rider to improve their balance when jumping. It prevents them from getting ahead of the movement and 'jumping before the horse', which is a bad fault as it restricts the movement of the forehand. It also stops them being behind the movement, which disturbs the horse's freedom of movement or fluidity.

Please note: in no circumstances should a novice ride without stirrups before they have total confidence in their horse and are completely calm. The safer the rider feels with stirrups, the sooner they will learn to trust the horse.

To start with the rider should take their feet out of the stirrups (leaving them hanging) after a fence and ride a circle or a volte. The moment they take their feet out of the stirrups, they will ride more 'with' their horse: they must relax the seat and 'swing' with the horse's movement more. Their legs should lengthen and the lower legs lie quietly against the horse's sides. Once the rider feels safe riding without stirrups, these can be removed from the saddle. (Leaving them hanging or crossing them over the horse's withers can disturb the horse.)

First ride over a single cavalletti, then two on a straight line (refer back to Exercise 1: Cantering over cavalletti on straight lines, page 86). Once the rider is used to this, they can ride a small grid (at a low height to start with). Going over fences in quick succession like this gives the rider time to get the feeling of being over the horse's centre of gravity.

The better balanced a rider is without the support of reins or stirrups, the safer, more supple and effective they will be.

It is important to ensure that the horse is happy and remains relaxed, and that the rider rides with feel, concentrating on going with the movement of the horse.

## Schooling the horse

### Equipment

Apart from a jumping saddle, all that is needed is a bridle, perhaps a martingale, and leg protection. When jumping, the horse's legs should be protected from injury with open-fronted jumping boots on the forelegs and fetlock boots behind. Open-fronted jumping boots protect the tendons, but allow the horse to feel if he knocks a pole, which teaches him to be careful. Overreach boots can be used on the front legs of

The correct equipment for a jumping horse.

horses who tend to catch the back of the shoes on the front feet with the hind feet.

The horse should wear the same bridle for jumping that he does for dressage. For daily training, the bit should not be too thin and sharp. Many riders resort to using a more severe bit when difficulties in training occur, instead of correcting problems with schooling. Better results are achieved by schooling the horse quietly and patiently.

In some cases, an advanced rider may experiment with a sharper bit at home; one that they may use later on when competing. For horses with especially sensitive mouths, a bit with a double-jointed (French link-style) mouthpiece can be useful. A martingale will prevent the horse from throwing his head up too high, but it should not interfere with the contact between the rider's hand and the horse's mouth. Variations in tack depend on the rideability and submissiveness of the horse.

## Before starting

As already explained, the rider is responsible for selecting a good line of approach and establishing a suitable tempo. Before reaching the first element of a grid (cavalletti or small jumps) their hands must be moved forwards in the direction of the horse's mouth. This so the horse is not unbalanced during the exercise and learns to jump for himself.

Before jumping training can begin the horse should be responsive to the rider's aids and trust the rider enough to relax, work through the back, in a rhythm, and respond willingly to halts and transitions. Before the young horse is ridden over his first fence, he should be used to free-jumping, cavalletti work and trotting over coloured poles.

A good jumping seat with the heels down and the hands low.

*Below*

The grid will be constructed one element at a time after the four cavalletti.

One of the most important aspects of training a young horse to jump is the landing phase, when the horse must be ridden forwards after the jump. At this point, the horse must learn to concentrate entirely on the rider. He should learn to wait for the rider's aids after the jump, not simply rush away in an uncontrolled manner. Initially, to keep the horse under control, the rider should keep him on a straight line and ride a transition to trot, progressing to walk or halt at a later stage in training. Circles and voltes can also be ridden, changing direction frequently.

To get the horse used to different situations, the approach should be ridden alternately – once from the left rein, once from the right rein.

> **Monotony prevents learning.**

Gymnastic jumping requires a lot of concentration and attentiveness from the horse, so it is important to take frequent breaks when the rider feels the horse needs them.

In my experience, there should be no fixed regime laid down about how often, or for how long, young horses should be jumped. On one hand, the horse learns by frequent repetition (for example, grid work), but on the other hand he can become bored by too much repetition. In the worst cases, after doing the same thing for too long time after time, the horse can become careless and lose concentration. Changes in the training routine are up to the rider: the aim being to ensure the horse enjoys jumping and can cope with the training.

Gymnastic jumping varies from horse to horse, and depends on temperament, length of the canter strides, jumping technique and rideability and on how much the horse actually enjoys jumping. It is important that the rider and the trainer work together to plan the best jump layouts to suit the individual horse. The next section has information on how to build fences to help novice horses without overfacing them or asking for too much too soon.

Before work commences, the jump stands should be set out at exactly the right distances for the horse, and the poles should be laid beside the stands, on the ground to one side of the grid, to make building the jumps quick and easy. Three or four poles or cavalletti can be laid at the beginning of the row of jumps and used for loosening up. It is useful to have two to four extra poles to hand that can be used as wings.

For safety's sake, the distance between jumps should be measured exactly.

With grid work, fences are jumped in **quick succession** one after the other.

## Grids for novice horses

The inexperienced young horse should learn that he must jump over every fence from the start. He must accept that there is no way out, and must not be given the chance to run out or to refuse. Once the horse understands this, jumping will be fun. From a practical point of view, this means that the rider must ride their horse positively over the first fence (from walk if necessary). A timid horse needs a lot of vocal encouragement, or you could take a lead from an experienced horse. Once the horse learns to jump one fence willingly with confidence, then he can begin grid work (jumping a series of fences in a row).

It is important to keep things simple when constructing jumps.

Wings may be used with novice horses. The first fence should be placed against the wall or fence, to prevent the horse from running out to one side, and jumped towards the exit, where the horse will naturally want to go.

Being allowed to smell the jump-building material helps the young horse to gain in confidence and trust.

Remember that there must always be a *loosening up phase*. In this case, the horse should also be allowed to investigate, and to smell, different jump-building materials to build his trust and confidence. The following jump layouts can be used for the *work phase*.

For every *upright* fence, use two poles, plus another laid as a ground line at a distance of about 30cm in front of the fence to help a novice horse to take off at the correct distance.

Every *oxer* should be constructed from three poles, with the ground line pole laid under the front rail of the oxer, so it cannot roll away. The oxer poles should be the same height as each other. Alternatively, the back pole can be one or two holes higher as an easier option.

An experienced horse gives a youngster a lead.

In the early stages, where the horse is getting used to jumping, only simple building materials should be used. Jump fillers are too distracting. The jumps should, however, be as wide as possible – about 3.5m.

Between the obstacles, you can lay ground poles. Use cavalletti or planks to keep them still. I have known a horse to be injured when he stood on a pole that rolled.

I reiterate that with a young horse it is particularly important to jump with care. The first time the horse jumps, the rider must keep a light contact with the mouth. If the contact is released too soon, the horse will feel abandoned. In the beginning it is advisable to take the hands forwards along the crest of the mane. If the horse does anything unexpected, such as spooking or throwing his head up, the rider can simply hold the mane, or lean on the neck for support. The rider should not have too strong a contact over the fence. The horse must learn to trust the rider over the fence – only then will he round his back and stretch his neck forwards to balance.

This novice horse jumps calmly.

## A starter grid

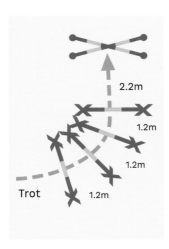

The diagram (left) shows a layout for starting grids with a novice horse. Place a pair of jump stands followed by three or four cavalletti around a corner; set them up off the track. The rider should ride in trot around the school, practising riding between the jump stands and aiming for the middle of the cavalletti, instead of continuing on the track. The cavalletti on the corner can prevent the horse from rushing when a jump is put into position. Eventually they will no longer be needed.

Once the horse is able to trot calmly over the cavalletti at their lowest height without any problems, a higher cavalletti or cross pole fence (using the stands) can be added at a distance of 2.2m. Wings and the wall or fence prevent the horse from running out. Should he refuse, the jumps are low enough for him to be asked to hop over them from walk, or even halt.

Cavalletti are placed on the corner before the grid to help the horse to concentrate.

After each successful attempt, the horse should be brought to a halt and praised. This is how to develop trust from the beginning.

A quiet voice and a pat on the neck help to calm the horse if he is a bit anxious. There are horses who concentrate so much on picking their feet up over the cavalletti that they try to trot over the higher obstacle at the end. In this situation, a small cross pole may be better since it will encourage the horse to jump.

*Sequence below*

1   The horse jumps over the cross pole.

2   Then the upright.

3   The blue cross pole will eventually become an oxer.

The next stage is to place a pole or cavalletti at a distance of 3m after the cross pole fence to encourage the horse to take a canter stride, after going over the cross pole. Later, this can be replaced with a small upright fence.

There are no hard and fast rules as to how many elements should be added to the grid, and when. But the grid should be added to in easy stages, so that it only takes the horse two or three attempts to get it right before moving on to the next step. For example, when adding an oxer, put a pole on the ground first, then make a small upright, before adding a back pole to turn the jump into a spread.

If the horse is too slow, he should canter forwards on the other long side, and be steadied on the corner before the jumps.

The number of cavalletti before the grid should be reduced from three to one when appropriate to maintain fluency.

Two to three days later, try another session, this time placing a pole on the ground after the higher cavalletti/cross pole at a distance of 3m, where an upright will later be built. The grid will be built up step by step as follows: after the upright another ground pole should be placed at a distance of 3m followed by another at a distance of 3.2m, which will become another upright, followed by a pole at 3.3m, which will become an oxer.

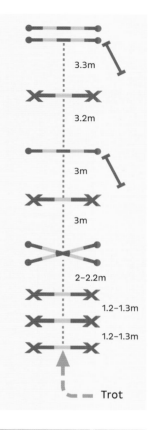

3.3m

3.2m

3m

3m

2–2.2m

1.2–1.3m

1.2–1.3m

Trot

*Right* **The jumping grid should be built up step by step.**

Building the grid in this way ensures that the horse remains confident as the elements are added. Should he refuse or run out, he should follow a lead horse a few times, and then try again alone.

To finish, the rider could go over a separate upright fence with a ground pole laid 2.2m in front of it. Start by doing it like this: at the end of the grid, bring the horse back into trot, before jumping the separate upright fence from trot. Then do a transition to halt. The grid can then be done again. In this way, a schooling routine is built up, using the whole school.

When a second fence is added to the grid, it is important to place a ground pole in front of the preceding upright, especially for young horses. They will tend to focus on the new fence, so the ground pole will help them to continue to jump the first upright without making mistakes.

## Grid work on the centre line

The advantage of constructing a grid on the centre line is that it can be jumped on both reins without having to make any alterations to the layout. The horse has to jump the first fence of the grid on the centre line without the support of the wall or fence. In the beginning, wings can be used to prevent running out.

The grid starts with three or four cavalletti: the turn onto the centre line must be accurate enough to ride over the middle of these. They are followed by a cross pole at a distance of about 2.2m. To begin with, the poles of the jumps on the long sides are laid on the ground, so the rider can use the whole school. After jumping the cross pole, the rider should turn at the end of the centre line in the direction of whichever canter lead the horse is on, and halt in the corner. After a few attempts, the rider should aim to halt on the centre line after the fence, keeping the horse straight.

The next stage is to put the poles for the oxer and small upright in place but on the ground. As described above, build the oxer first as an upright and then as a spread. Constructing the grid gradually ensures that the horse remains confident and able to do what is being asked.

This time, after the grid, the rider trots on the right rein on the inside track, going over the poles on the ground. After jumping the grid the next time, the rider turns to the left, going over poles for the small oxer. The jump stands for the back rail should be close to the front ones, so the

*Opposite page above*

This grid layout is very useful for young horses. The single jumps are built on the track on the long sides. Wings are used to prevent the horse from running out.

*Opposite page below*

1   The horse is relaxed as he trots over the cavalletti …

2   … approaches the cross pole …

3   … and jumps straight over it.

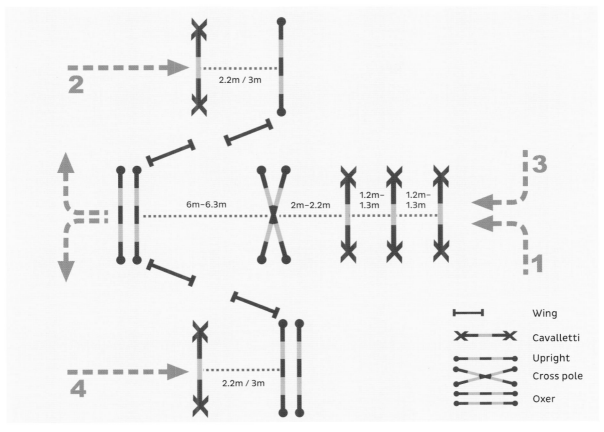

2.2m / 3m

6m–6.3m    2m–2.2m    1.2m–1.3m    1.2m–1.3m

3

1

4    2.2m / 3m

| | Wing |
| --- | --- |
| | Cavalletti |
| | Upright |
| | Cross pole |
| | Oxer |

oxer will not be too wide. The two jumps can then be built, both with cavalletti or poles on the ground 3m before them.

The complete exercise can then build up as follows: the rider approaches the centre line in trot and canters on the right lead, turning to the right after the grid (if the horse picks up left lead canter, a change of leg should be made through trot) and jumps over the upright. A transition to trot should be made before the corner and the grid on the centre line ridden again; this time the turn is to the left to jump the oxer. A short rest can now be taken.

## Grid work on the diagonals

With the layout shown opposite or any diagonal grid, the main issue is to keep the horse straight.

To start with, put all the jump stands in place with the poles laid to the sides. The three to four cavalletti on each of the diagonals can be ridden in trot as part of the warm up.

The grid starts with a cross pole at a distance of 2m or 2.2m from the last cavalletti. The rider trots on the first diagonal, steadies up, then continues around the whole school before turning onto the second diagonal and continuing around the whole school again. (This is the repeated route: diagonal, whole school, diagonal, whole school.) The next step is to build an upright at a distance of 6–6.3m and then, later, an oxer.

The horse should then have a break in walk on a long rein, if not sooner.

During this break, build an upright and an oxer on the long sides of the school. If it is felt useful for the horse, a low cavalletti or ground pole can be laid 3m before each of these fences, and/or wings added if necessary.

With some horses (especially those who become bored easily) the number of trot cavalletti can be reduced to one, to make the approach to the first fence less demanding. A single cavalletti helps to keep the horse straight and prevents him from running out. The second fence is enclosed by the other jumps, which also prevents the horse from running out.

Eventually, the whole exercise can be put together as follows: the rider begins on the left rein in trot, turning onto the diagonal (1), trots over the cavalletti and the cross pole, canters one stride and jumps the upright. They proceed in right lead canter (the canter lead should be corrected if the horse is on the wrong leg) and canter over the middle of the upright fence on the long side (2). The rider then brings the horse back to trot, turns onto the next diagonal (3), trots over the cavalletti and the cross pole, canters for a stride and jumps the oxer. In left canter, the horse should now go around the school to jump the oxer on the long side (4).

If this successful, give the horse a break. The rider should make sure that the horse maintains the canter rhythm throughout the exercise and remains straight before, over and after each jump. If he becomes excited and too strong, the rider should ride a circle or a volte.

Parts of the exercise can be repeated as necessary to build trust and confidence in the horse.

In the early stages of grid work for the horse, the fences can be built either on the track, or on the centre line. The former has the advantage that the wall or fence helps to prevent the horse from running out to one

This layout helps to prevent the horse from running out.

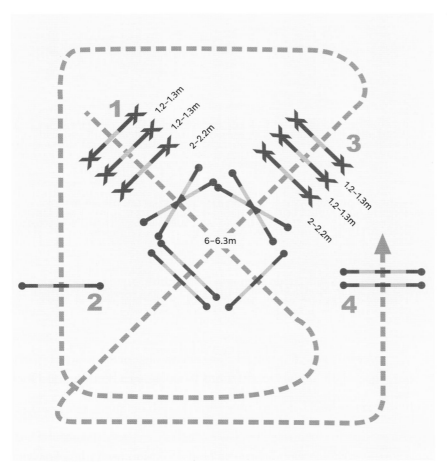

side. The disadvantage is that it is not possible to ride freely around the whole school on the track.

Building the grid on the centre line allows the rider to ride around the whole school on both reins. The single jumps on the long sides can be ridden on both reins (build the oxer as a parallel). Position them on the inside track so it is possible to ride past them on the track.

Remember to loosen up the horse before starting to jump. The rider can then start working through the grid. When the horse has jumped willingly, and straight, through each part of the grid a couple of times, the next element can be added.

It is important that the distances between the fences accurately match the length of the horse's canter stride so he remains relaxed through his back when he jumps. He should jump over the four obstacles without having to change the length of his stride. If the horse stops before a fence or tries to run out, approach and jump the single fences from a circle, before finally repeating the whole grid.

This novice horse jumps carefully over an oxer.

There are horses who can lose co-ordination when jumping fences in close succession, one after the other. With these it is pointless repeating the grid again and again. It is far better to take a short break and then try again with a simplified version before doing the whole thing.

Bear in mind that if the horse becomes too strong, you can steady him by placing a ground pole midway between each obstacle.

Using cross poles for this small oxer helps the horse to jump over the centre of the fence.

## Bounces

Bounces (or in-and-outs) are obstacles without a canter stride in between: after landing, the horse must take off straight away to get over the next fence. Once the horse is used to grid work, small bounces are very useful for improving the swing through the horse's back. They are a very effective way of increasing suppleness and dexterity, and a valuable gymnastic exercise. They also improve concentration. However, this work can be strenuous. Avoid the risk of straining the horse by keeping the fences low and do not repeat them too many times.

Bounce in ...

... and bounce out ...

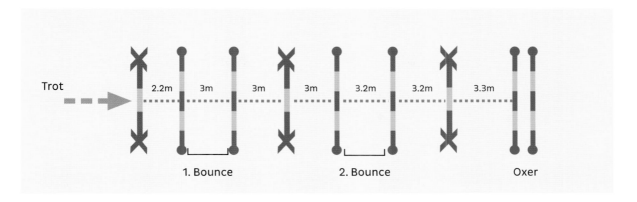

Trot

2.2m · 3m · 3m · 3m · 3.2m · 3.2m · 3.3m

1. Bounce          2. Bounce          Oxer

*Above*

A grid with two bounces and an oxer.

... over the oxer.

The whole grid from the front.

You can build a bounce with two cavalletti at their highest height or with two cross pole fences. To get the correct stride from the horse, it can help to lay one ground pole or a low cavalletti 2.2m in front of the first fence, and another 3–3.3m after the second. This also helps the horse to get the idea of what to do.

The individual jumps should be small and the same height. If the horse copes with two fences easily, another element can be added, which will also help him get used to adjusting to new situations as they are presented.

The rider should ride the approach on a bend so the horse does not get overexcited when confronted by a mass of poles.

## A bounce grid with cross poles

A variation of this bounce grid is to use a series of cross poles, which help the horse to jump over the centre of each jump.

Devising grids of this type depends very much on the horse. You could start using a series of poles on the ground or low cavalletti, building a cross pole at a distance of 2.2m after the last cavalletti. Further cross poles can be added one at a time. Another option is to place all the jump stands where they are required, with the poles on the ground between them, and build them up one at a time into cross pole fences. Put a cavalletti at a distance of 2.2m from the last cross pole to enable the grid to be ridden from both directions, facilitating a change of rein.

To progress from this, the low cavalletti, or ground pole, can be rolled further away from the first and the last cross poles to a distance of 3m so it can be ridden in canter. As this distance is short the horse must step

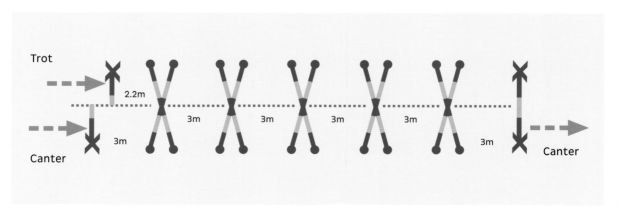

A bounce grid with cross poles.

under his centre of gravity in order to push off the ground with more power. The exercise can be ridden with up to five cross poles, but for young horses use just three – as always depending on the horse. There is a risk of asking too much if you use more than five.

Schooling over bounces is very good for getting the horse fit, but increase the work in increments to avoid asking too much too soon and upsetting him.

As the horse's concentration increases, so does his self-awareness and his confidence. He will also learn to be careful and to have faster reflexes. This is important from a safety point of view when you are planning to ride a horse over a show jumping course or cross-country.

1 Start with small cross poles.

2 Place a cavalletti after the last cross pole to encourage the horse to canter forwards after the grid.

1 The horse starts by jumping crookedly over the higher part of the first cross pole.

2 As he goes through the grid, he straightens and jumps over the centre of the cross poles.

Jumping bounces also improves the horse's bascule and leg technique, skills of particular importance for the jumping horse. I must emphasise again that is it very important not to overtax your horse when doing this type of work. You must make sure that you have his full attention and that he is fit enough to do what you are asking, and remember always to finish on a good note. Varying the exercises will keep him keen and maintain a positive attitude.

This useful exercise improves co-ordination and concentration.

## More layouts for grid work

There are endless variations on grid layouts. You can build them specifically to improve the rider's seat, increase the horse's impulsion, and to help with many training problems. The two grid layouts shown on these pages are just a start. (For more ideas see 'Common problems and ways to correct them' pages 122–129).

When introducing canter grids, the rider should be confident approaching the grid in trot before making the approach in canter.

I am not going to go into too many technical details – my aim here is to focus on building a solid foundation for future schooling. For more details on training, see the jumping section of my book *Basic Training of the Young Horse*.

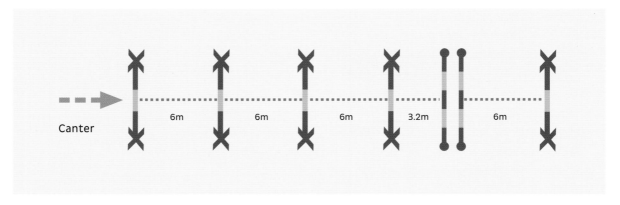

Canter

6m    6m    6m    3.2m    6m

Grid layout to improve rhythm.

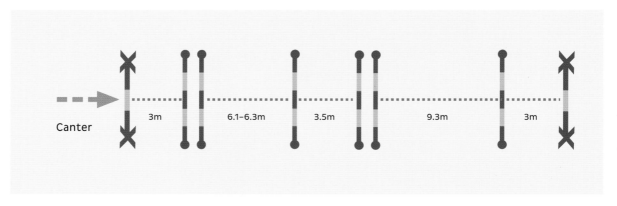

Canter

3m    6.1–6.3m    3.5m    9.3m    3m

A progressive grid.

With the rider in a lovely balanced seat, the horse is able to perform a good bascule.

1/2 This horse canters rhythmically over the cavalletti ...

3 ... and jumps in good style over the oxer.

## Common problems and ways to correct them

**PROBLEM >**

The horse gets strong after the last jump, bucking or running away.

**CORRECTION >**

After landing, maintain a soft contact and use the voice to steady the horse (if he bucks, keep his head up and, for safety's sake, lean back). Turning onto a circle and/or a volte will help. In my opinion, stopping a horse abruptly by the wall, which is often done, is not a good idea, as this can make the horse unsure of himself, destroying his self-confidence.

Do half-halts, making sure you keep your hands gentle. If the horse has a sore mouth from being ridden with rough hands, he will become tense when jumping and be afraid of the contact.

An alternative is to enlist someone's help, asking them to stand in line with the jump, their arms outstretched to discourage the horse from running off. The rider should stop in front of the person – who should not take any risks with their own safety.

Use the following exercise to bring the horse under control after the fence: trot or canter over a small fence (a cavalletti is ideal) towards the wall and then ride on a figure of eight until the horse accepts the aids and can be brought quietly back under control.

This rider sits against the movement and prevents the horse from rounding his back over the cavalletti.

This layout shows how to arrange two cavalletti so that they can be jumped towards a wall or fence. This helps to bring the horse back under control.

## PROBLEM >

The horse rushes towards the grid.

## CORRECTION >

Place three to four cavalletti around a corner, and put the first element of the grid directly after the corner, so the horse has to concentrate on keeping his balance.

Ride the corner a few times, and either turn away before the grid, or bring the horse to a halt before the first jump, then rein-back for a horse's length before turning away again. The horse *must* be kept on the aids. It is easier to bring a horse like this to a halt in front of the fence if you can get someone to stand in the way (again, bearing safety in mind).

Trot cavalletti laid around the corner will prevent the horse rushing towards the grid.

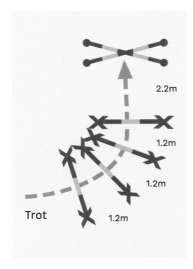

PROBLEM >

The horse becomes gets too fast and out of control halfway through the grid.

CORRECTION >

Ask someone to move from side to side between the jumps (or after the last jump, which may be easier) so the horse concentrates on the person and forgets about rushing off.

PROBLEM >

The horse jumps flat and is careless and inattentive.

CORRECTION >

Place the top poles so they slant alternately through the grid. This gives the horse more to look at, keeps him alert and should prevent him from making mistakes.

Someone moving from side to side after the last fence can also help.

If the horse makes a mistake, the rider should sit quietly and not over-react. Horses learn from making mistakes, becoming more careful when they jump. In short, mistakes make them more aware.

Sloping the top rail of an obstacle makes a horse pay more attention.

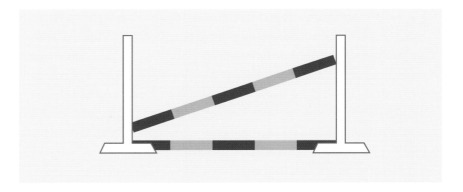

PROBLEM >

The horse always runs out to one particular side. In this example we'll say it's to the left.

CORRECTION >

Holding your whip and the horse's mane in the left hand, bring your right hand out to the side and turn the horse to the right. Before the jump, tap the horse once with the whip, and turn him once all the away around to the right before approaching the fence again from the right rein. Problem solved!

**PROBLEM >**

The horse is crooked before and after the jump.

**CORRECTION >**

Place two poles at right angles to the fence to make guides to lead the horse into the fence. They should be far enough apart so as not to distract him. Once he is used to the guides, move them even closer together to

1 Pairs of poles are laid to form a guide to the jump.

2 Single poles are laid on the horse's 'problem' side.

keep him in the centre of the fence. Another option is to place poles on the ground before and after the fence.

The guides can also be laid as a V, either on the ground or with the ends of the poles leaning on the fence. In the example shown here, the poles are leant against the front rail of an oxer.

1 The horse is crooked on the approach ...

2 ... but straightens up over the middle of the fence between the V-shaped poles.

**PROBLEM ❯**

The horse jumps crookedly and lands over to one side. It is important that a horse lands straight after the fence because this also ensures that the bascule is correct. Turning in the air can cause a variety of problems.

**CORRECTION >**

Lay a pole after the fence, putting it on the side towards which the horse lands (see photos below). It must be far enough away from the fence that there is no risk of the horse landing on it. On landing, he should remain parallel to the pole when taking the first canter stride.

For example, if the horse always drifts to the left and lands left-of-centre after the fence, a pole should be laid 2–3m after the fence on the left side. Make sure the pole is in line with the fence wing to start with and then gradually roll it nearer to the middle of the fence as the horse gets used to it being there.

As necessary, you can place side poles throughout the grid, or work on correcting the crookedness with a single fence.

Another option is to lay a pole before and after the fence on different sides. Ride in a straight line over the middle of the fence, turn, and come back over it from the other direction.

Or you can make a lane with two poles both before and after the jump. This helps the horse to remain straight on the approach and the landing.

1 The horse twists and jumps to the right over the fence.

2 The horse notices the poles and corrects himself over the fence.

While the exercises given to correct crookedness when jumping can be useful, if the problem is marked/persistent it may be worthwhile investigating whether there are underlying physical reasons.

A cavalletti before and after the fence makes it easier for horse and rider to jump fluently.

**PROBLEM >**

The horse finds it difficult to work out the correct take-off point.

**CORRECTION >**

Place a cavalletti in front of an upright fence (it must be at least the same width as the fence). Concentrating on the cavalletti before the fence will help the horse to relax and to round his back over the jump. Another option is to place a take-off pole 3–3.2m before the fence. This helps the horse to adjust his canter stride to take off at the right distance from the fence.

Placing a cavalletti 3m after the jump will help the horse to land in the right place and prevents him from turning too suddenly after the jump. This exercise is very useful as it can be ridden on both reins in canter.

These examples give an idea of how varied grid work can be and how many options there are. Exercises can be devised to suit any horse and rider combination. There are innumerable possibilities.

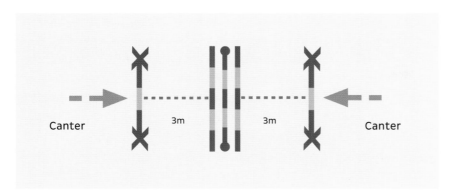

A cavalletti before and after the fence.

Remember that every exercise must be done with care and calmness. Do not forget to reward the horse as soon as he has done well.

I hope that this chapter will encourage riders and instructors to use gymnastic jumping in their training and appreciate the variety it can bring to the horse's daily schooling regime.

# CHAPTER 7

# TRAINING PROGRAMMES

## Basic rules

A training programme is simply a starting point for working out a holistic regime for the horse, making sure that all aspects of his schooling are covered on a regular basis. This chapter is intended as a guide to putting together this sort of programme. The options given include information on how and when to use cavalletti and gymnastic jumping. Other aspects of training can fit loosely around these. It is, of course, vital that each training programme is adapted to suit the individual horse.

The following programmes could all be used in basic training and as a stepping stone to future work. They outline approaches for a variety of systematic training regimes.

It is important to take into account seasonal differences. For example, in summer, many riders go to competitions or hack out, and in winter they concentrate more on schooling. The programmes can be adapted to take this into account since they have a short time scale of between four and six weeks.

Ideas are also given for individual schooling sessions, which the rider can adapt accordingly.

Every lesson should be divided into three parts: loosening up and cooling off at the beginning and end, and in between the work phase when the exercises are ridden. Loosening up over cavalletti should last for about 10–15 minutes. The total length of a schooling session depends on the conformation, age, temperament, keenness and rideability of your horse. Cooling off in walk on a long rein is vital for calming the horse so he returns to the stable happy and relaxed. This should last for about 10 minutes.

Cavalletti or grids should be done in the middle of the schooling session.

## Four to six week plan for basic training

This programme is for horses in their second year of training. The basic training of the riding horse should cover all areas of horsemanship. The aim of this plan is to prepare the horse to compete at the lowest level. Although you should already have thought about which equestrian discipline you want to specialise in, the way to reach any equestrian goal is to have a sound basic training in as many areas as possible.

### FIRST WEEK

**Aim** – Familiarisation with work over cavalletti in walk and trot and some basic gymnastic jumping exercises.

### Monday
Day off. However, the horse should not stand all day in the stable but should be walked in hand for at least 30 minutes. If possible he could be turned out, ridden out in walk or given some time to wander around in the school or paddock.

### Tuesday

▶ Begin with cavalletti work without the rider for about 30 minutes. Choosing:

*Option A* Loose schooling – phase 1 and 2 (pages 24–5) – 15 minutes, phase 3 (page 26) – 15 minutes.

*Option B* On the lunge – phase 1 and 2 (page 32) – 15 minutes, phase 3 (pages 35–8) – 15 minutes.

▶ About 10 minutes riding over cavalletti in walk (page 42).

▶ Finish with dressage and cooling off.

Cavalletti work in walk on a straight line.

## Wednesday

▶ Loosening up in walk, trot and canter for about 15 minutes.

▶ Followed by 20 minutes ridden cavalletti work on straight lines, first in walk, starting with one pole (page 42), then in trot (pages 48–60) with 5 minutes rest in between.

▶ Finish with dressage and cooling off.

## Thursday

▶ No cavalletti work. Depending on the weather, go for a quiet hack or ride a dressage session as relaxed and quietly as possible.

## Friday

▶ Loosen up for at least 10 minutes.

▶ No more than 30 minutes ridden cavalletti work on straight lines, first in walk, increasing the distance between the poles for medium walk (pages 44–45). Repeat in trot, increasing the distance towards the end of the session, with a 5 minute break in between.

▶ Some dressage exercises in canter or working in canter in a light seat, on both reins. Finish with a few jumps from trot and canter on straight lines, then cool off.

**Saturday**
As Thursday.

**Sunday**

▶ Depending on the weather, choose:

*Option A* Hack out jumping over small, natural obstacles, hill work, quiet canter over uneven ground.

*Option B* In the school: loosening up, dressage exercises to improve throughness, followed by cantering on both reins in a light seat, finishing with a few jumps out of trot and canter.

**SECOND WEEK**

**Aim** – To establish what was learnt in the first week.

**Monday**
Day off (or as before).

**Tuesday**

▶ A good 15 minutes loosening up, riding in walk on a long rein over cavalletti on straight lines.

▶ About 20 minutes in walk and trot over cavalletti on straight lines, increasing the number of cavalletti if possible.

▶ A few dressage exercises in canter, cool off.

**Wednesday**
As Thursday the first week.

**Thursday**

▶ Loosen up for about 15 minutes.

Trot on straight lines over more cavalletti.

▶ No more than 30 minutes ridden cavalletti work in walk and trot. Do the concentration exercise (page 59) and extended walk (page 45), with a short break of 5 minutes in between.

▶ A little dressage or cantering in a light seat on both reins, finishing with a few jumps from trot and canter on straight lines; cool off.

## Friday
As Thursday the first week.

## Saturday

▶ Free-jumping or cavalletti work without the rider, loose schooling or on the lunge, or as Thursday the second week.

▶ Dressage.

▶ Cool off.

## Sunday
As Sunday the first week or as Thursday the second week.

## THIRD WEEK

**Aim** – Familiarisation with ground poles in canter and basic gymnastic jumping.

### Monday
Day off.

### Tuesday
As Tuesday the second week.

### Wednesday

▶ About 15 minutes loosening up.

▶ No more than 15 minutes cavalletti work in trot on straight lines.

▶ About 8 minutes cantering in a light seat on both reins; finish with basic gymnastic jumping exercises on a straight line.

▶ Cool off.

### Thursday
As Thursday the first week.

### Friday

▶ About 15 minutes loosening up.

▶ Dressage exercises to improve throughness.

▶ Basic gymnastic jumping exercises.

▶ Cool off.

### Saturday
As Thursday the first week.

### Sunday

▶ About 15 minutes loosening up, including walking over cavalletti on a long rein, on straight lines.

▶ About 10 minutes cantering in a light seat on both reins, with a 5-minute rest in walk.

Trot on straight lines over more cavalletti.

▶ Basic gymnastic jumping exercises on a straight line.

▶ Cool off.

### FOURTH WEEK

**Aim** – To reinforce what was learnt in the third week.

**Monday**
Day off.

**Tuesday**
No cavalletti work; ride dressage with a long loosening up phase.

### Wednesday
As Wednesday or Friday the third week.

### Thursday
As Tuesday.

### Friday
As Sunday the third week.

### Saturday
Hacking out, depending on the weather, or dressage.

### Sunday

▶ 15 minutes loosening up.

▶ Basic gymnastic exercises over cavalletti, poles and a single jump, or a round of show jumps.

A variation on gymnastic jumping on a straight line.

## FIFTH WEEK

No cavalletti work, but more dressage and, when possible, hacking out.

## SIXTH WEEK

Repeat the most important exercises from the first four weeks, or increase their difficulty.

After the sixth week, the horse should be confident with all the basic cavalletti work on straight lines and the gymnastic jumping. From the seventh week, adjust the work to aim for your particular goal. From now on, you can include cavalletti work on circles.

The first six weeks of work will have prepared the horse for further training, and he should not find it difficult. It is normal for problems to occur from time to time during training. Most are rectified with loosening work and going back to simpler exercises. The difficulty of any exercise must be slowly increased once the basics have been well established.

Trotting uphill brings an element of fun into the training regime, and builds condition.

# Four to six week plan for a dressage horse

This programme follows on from basic training. Cavalletti work is very versatile and can be applied to all the basic training. Its use is only limited by the imagination of the rider. What the exercises are used for depends on the individual dressage horse. Every good dressage book emphasises the importance of training dressage movements step-by-step.

## FIRST WEEK

### Monday
Day off.

### Tuesday
▶ About 20 minutes loosening up exercises on both reins in all three gaits, finishing with trot and walk over cavalletti on straight lines.

▶ Exercises to improve suppleness using transitions and walking on a long rein over cavalletti, to improve the clarity of the walk rhythm.

▶ Riding forwards in trot.

▶ Cool off.

### Wednesday
No cavalletti work.

### Thursday
▶ Cavalletti work in trot, finishing with lengthening the strides (page 56) to improve swing, impulsion and ground cover.

### Friday
No cavalletti work.

### Saturday
▶ No cavalletti work, except for loosening up over cavalletti on a long rein, or free-schooling over cavalletti (page 26), or free jumping.

### Sunday
▶ Take part in a test, or ride the movements from a dressage test.

Riding forwards-downwards over cavalletti to loosen the horse.

## SECOND WEEK

### Monday
Day off.

### Tuesday
No cavalletti work.

### Wednesday

▶ Cavalletti work in walk over shorter distances to improve collected walk (pages 46–7).

### Thursday
No cavalletti work.

### Friday

▶ No cavalletti work, except for loosening up over cavalletti in rising trot on straight lines.

### Saturday

► Cavalletti work in trot, finishing in sitting trot over shortened distances to improve pushing power (impulsion) (page 51).

### Sunday

► Take part in a test, or ride the movements from a dressage test.

## THIRD WEEK

### Monday
Day off.

### Tuesday

► Free-schooling over cavalletti (pages 26–9).

### Wednesday
No cavalletti work.

Riding dressage movements out on a hack.

### Thursday

▶ No cavalletti work except for loosening up on a long rein.

### Friday

As Thursday the first week.

### Saturday

No cavalletti work.

### Sunday

▶ Take part in a test, or ride the movements from a dressage test.

## FOURTH WEEK

### Monday

Day off.

### Tuesday

As Tuesday the first week.

### Wednesday

No cavalletti work.

### Thursday

▶ Cavalletti work in walk, finishing with wider distances to improve ground cover.

### Friday

No cavalletti work.

### Saturday

As Saturday the second week.

### Sunday

▶ Take part in a test, or ride the movements from a dressage test.

Relaxation for horse and rider.

Hacking out in a group is great fun.

### FIFTH WEEK

No cavalletti work; concentrate on dressage, loosening up by hacking out.

### SIXTH WEEK

Repeat the most important exercises from the first three weeks, as well as some of the exercises from basic training.

Cavalletti work on circles can also be introduced. On days that you have problems, remember to simplify the exercises, and repeat the session the next day. Aim to do cavalletti work only two or three times a week to avoid the risk of asking too much, resulting in strain or injury.

# Four to six week plan for a jumping horse

Again, this work follows on from basic training.

## FIRST WEEK

### Monday
Day off.

### Tuesday
▶ A long loosening up session with cavalletti work in rising trot on straight lines.

▶ Canter work in a light seat.

▶ A few exercises to improve responses to the aids.

▶ Cool off.

### Wednesday
▶ Loosening up.

▶ Exercises to improve responses to the aids.

▶ Gymnastic jumping, finishing with one or two single obstacles.

▶ Cool off.

### Thursday
▶ Dressage or hacking, depending on the weather.

### Friday
▶ Dressage with a few single jumps, or related distances out of canter.

### Saturday
▶ Hacking out with hill work and cantering steadily over uneven ground, depending on the weather, or dressage.

### Sunday
▶ Related distances on straight and curved lines.

Bounces build strength ...

## SECOND WEEK

**Monday**
Day off

**Tuesday**

▶ Loosening work.

▶ Some exercises to improve throughness.

▶ Cantering in a light seat over cavalletti or small jumps.

▶ Cool off.

**Wednesday**

▶ Choose:

*Option A* cavalletti work – free schooling, finishing with dressage.

*Option B* long loosening up session with cavalletti work in trot on curved lines; canter work to improve the quality of the canter; cool off.

**Thursday**

▶ Gymnastic jumping.

**Friday**

▶ Dressage.

**Saturday**

▶ Jumping a course.

**Sunday**
Day off.

... and increase concentration.

*Opposite page*

Gymnastic jumping improves the balance of both rider and horse.

## THIRD WEEK

### Monday
As Tuesday the first week.

### Tuesday

▶ More difficult gymnastic jumping.

### Wednesday
As Tuesday the second week.

### Thursday
As Thursday the first week.

### Friday

▶ Cavalletti work in canter, and jumping combination fences.

### Saturday

▶ Loosening up.

▶ Canter work to improve condition on both reins with a break in between in walk.

▶ Cooling off and calming down by riding over cavalletti on straight lines, in walk on a long rein.

### Sunday

▶ Jumping part of a show jumping course with fences in a variety of styles and colours.

## FOURTH WEEK

### Monday
Day off.

### Tuesday

▶ Depending on the weather, choosing:

*Option A*  a long loosening up session on a hack, finishing with dressage.

*Option B*  as Tuesday the first or second week.

Riding out is good for the soul.

## Wednesday

As Wednesday the first week.

## Thursday

▶ Dressage.

## Friday

▶ Riding a variety of related distanced on circles.

## Saturday

As Thursday the first week.

## Sunday

▶ Jumping a course at a different venue.

### FIFTH WEEK

More dressage: perhaps one session of free-jumping, cavalletti work, competition-style jumps, maybe at a different venue.

### SIXTH WEEK

Repetition of the important exercises from the first three weeks, jumping combination fences – doubles and trebles.

## Ideas for young riders

When training children and teenagers, the main aim is to make sure they have fun, and develop confidence in their ponies or horses. A relaxed and flexible seat that moves with the horse can be learnt by hacking out, safely, and is the best preparation for later work. It is important that they also learn a correct dressage seat, which means they must learn to sit up

It's never too early to start...

straight from the very beginning. This seat is often misunderstood and instead of being elegant and elastic, the rider's position becomes rigid and stiff.

Cavalletti work is a good way of improving all aspects of riding. As I have said so many times throughout this book, the possibilities are endless and they give young riders in particular so much to concentrate on, that they will forget about being tense or worried.

# FURTHER READING

Eschbach, Andrea and Markus: **Riding Free,** J.A. Allen (London) and Trafalgar Square Books (USA), 2012.

Higgins, Gillian and Martin, Stephanie: **How Your Horse Moves**, David & Charles (UK), 2011.

Klimke, Ingrid and Reiner: **Basic Training of the Young Horse**, J.A. Allen (London) and Trafalgar Square Books (USA), 2006.

Loch, Sylvia: **Dressage – The Art of Classical Riding**, The Sportsman's Press (Quiller Books), 1990.

Meyners, Eckart: **Rider Fitness – Body and Brain**, Trafalgar Square Books (USA), 2011.

Paalman, Anthony: **Training Show Jumpers**, J.A.Allen (London), 1998.

Savoie, Jane: **That Winning Feeling!**, J.A. Allen (London) and Trafalgar Square Books (USA), 1999.

Schöffmann, Dr Britta: **Dressage Training Customized**, J.A. Allen (London) and Trafalgar Square Books (USA), 2010.

# INDEX